SPIRIT-LED BIBLE STUDY

THE GLORY OF GOD

GUILLERMO MALDONADO

WHITAKER
HOUSE

The Glory of God
(Spirit-Led Bible Study)

Guillermo Maldonado
13651 S.W. 143rd Ct., #101
Miami, FL 33186
http://kingjesusministry.org/
www.ERJPub.org

ISBN: 978-1-60374-564-2
Printed in the United States of America
© 2013 by Guillermo Maldonado

Whitaker House
1030 Hunt Valley Circle
New Kensington, PA 15068
www.whitakerhouse.com

1 2 3 4 5 6 7 8 9 10 11 ⨊ 20 19 18 17 16 15 14 13

CONTENTS

About the Spirit-Led Bible Study Series

The Spirit-Led Bible Study series is a collection of diverse, stand-alone Bible studies designed for either individuals or groups. Each self-study course features either a scriptural theme or a particular book of the Bible. Readers can go beyond just reading the Bible to become engaged in its truths and principles, learning to apply them to everyday life in practical ways while growing in their understanding of God and deepening their relationship with Him. Jesus said, *"When He, the Spirit of truth, has come, He will guide you into all truth"* (John 16:13). Readers are encouraged to recognize that it is only through the indwelling Holy Spirit that we may truly understand the Scriptures and exhibit the life of Christ in our lives, and that we must intentionally rely on the Spirit in all our reading and study of the Bible.

INTRODUCTION

I have met believers and leaders who constantly ask, "Is this all God has for me? Where is the God of power and miracles? Is Jesus just a historical figure or the living Christ? Can the Lord still do the same miracles the Bible talks about?"

God has not changed. He is the same yesterday, today, and forever. (See Hebrews 13:8.) I can testify from firsthand experience that God exists and continues to do miracles in our time, through His glory.

God's glory is not just a theoretical concept; it is spiritual truth. It is a heavenly reality that every believer can experience now. Mere "religion" will never produce a supernatural experience with God because it is void of the glory and life of the Lord. You can move beyond practicing religion to having an encounter with your heavenly Father—the Father of glory.

Without a continuous revelation of the glory of God, we will, sooner or later, get stuck in our ways and become as *"old wineskins"* (Luke 5:37). In other words, we will not allow God to do something new in our lives that would bring purpose, power, and healing. We are often so busy trying to keep up appearances and fulfill norms that we end up trapped in traditions. God wants us to return to His glory. He also wants to take us to new realms of His glory we've never experienced before.

Revealed knowledge introduces us to the dimension of glory, but hunger and thirst for God are what maintain us in it.

I always teach my congregation to follow the Miracle Maker, not the miracles. Our priority is to follow Jesus. When we do so, God will confirm His Word with signs. (See Mark 16:20.) I am passionate about seeing signs, miracles, and wonders, but my strongest passion is to know God and His glory in every respect and to become His instrument to impact the earth with the gospel in order to win souls.

I believe, preach, and practice theology that supports what the Bible teaches. I am a defender of the sound doctrine of Jesus Christ as Lord and Savior. And, as I have functioned in the scriptural role of apostle, I have learned to lay down a solid biblical foundation in the lives of thousands of new believers in my local church and around the world. Furthermore, I encourage the members of my leadership team to study biblical doctrine and to become established in it. I make this clarification so that no one will mistakenly assume that I reject or belittle doctrine or theology while promoting fresh revelation.

My apostolic calling is to teach, train, and equip believers. My heart's desire is not to be one of a small number of vessels God uses to perform His miracles, signs, and wonders but to equip thousands of leaders to train and guide others on the same path and to win souls. I have invested myself in the new generation that God is raising up, and I am witnessing amazing results. I want you to have the same results by combining your scriptural knowledge with revelation and allowing God to manifest His glory through you! The gospel of Jesus Christ is simple, practical, and powerful. Each of the following studies will help you to progress from foundational biblical doctrine to an exciting, purposeful life in which you experience the God of the Bible—the God of glory—every day as you become a carrier of His transforming, healing presence to the world.

But we all, with unveiled face, beholding as in a mirror the glory of the Lord, are being transformed into the same image from glory to glory, just as by the Spirit of the Lord.
(2 Corinthians 3:18)

HOW TO USE THIS STUDY

Introduction

Welcome to *The Glory of God*, part of the Spirit-Led Bible Study series. We are delighted that you have made the decision to dig deeper into God's Word. This course is designed as a stand-alone biblical study on the theme of God's glory. The study may be completed independently by individual students or may be used in a group setting, such as a Bible study, a Sunday school class, a course on the foundations of the Christian faith, or a prayer group. For those who have read the author's book *The Glory of God* (Whitaker House, 2012), this course reinforces its major themes while providing further scriptural study and application of the topic.

Elements of Each Study

Scripture Verse or Passage

Each study begins with a Scripture verse or passage that highlights the topic.

Introduction

The author provides background, context, and/or other relevant information to set the stage for the lesson that follows.

Study Questions

Each study includes approximately 20–35 questions, with some questions having multiple parts. The questions are organized under sections that emphasize particular aspects of the topic. Each question is followed by a corresponding Scripture reference in parentheses that enables the student to answer it. If a Scripture reference has *a* or *b* after it (e.g., "John 3:16a" or "John 3:16b"), this means the answer is found in the first part of the verse, "a," or the second part, "b." The student should read the Bible verse or passage and then either write the answer on the line(s) provided or circle the correct answer. Since this course gives a broad overview of the topic of the glory of God in the Bible, the student will be looking up a variety of relevant passages from both the Old and New Testaments.

Reflections

Each lesson includes insights that the author has gleaned from his experiences with God's glory in ministry and his study of the theme of glory in God's Word. For example, the first study features "Reflections on the Biblical Meaning of Glory."

Key Definitions

Definitions and explanations of key concepts related to God's glory are provided at various points throughout the studies.

Thought-Provoking Statements

Periodically, statements for personal reflection are presented in bold italics.

Conclusion

At the end of each study, the author sums up the topic and/or offers a challenge to the student.

Prayer of Activation

A prayer is provided to activate the students to live out the principles in the lesson, being spiritually empowered to serve God and receive from His glory. Group leaders are encouraged to offer the prayer on behalf of the students, while the individual student is encouraged to pray the prayer for himself or herself. (Individual students should adapt the prayers to the first-person singular.)

Action Steps

Action steps are listed to enable the student to apply the lesson to his or her life in practical ways.

Experiences with God's Glory

Each study concludes with a testimony about someone who has experienced a life-changing encounter with the glory of God through the author's church, King Jesus Ministry, in Miami, Florida, and the author's ministry in other countries.

Study Helps

Bible Version

The main Bible translation used for this study is the *New King James Version*. Other Bible translations are used periodically, and they are designated as follows:

(KJV): King James Version

(NIV): *New International Version*

Answer Key

At the back of this book, answers to the study questions are listed under the titles of the studies in the Answer Key section. In addition, the various section titles for each study are included for easy reference. The student's answers should reflect the content of those provided in the Answer Key, although the wording may differ slightly.

Study 1

OUR GLORIOUS GOD

*"Yours, O LORD, is the greatness, the power and the glory, the victory and the majesty;
for all that is in heaven and in earth is Yours; Yours is the kingdom, O LORD,
and You are exalted as head over all."*
—1 Chronicles 29:11

Introduction

The glory of God is not just a theological concept to be learned. It is a reality that can be experienced continually by His people. When we live in God's glory, we dwell in His very presence, receive His love and grace, understand His heart, learn His will, and experience His divine power. That power transforms lives—saving, healing, and delivering—and enacts miracles and wonders that reveal God's majesty.

Unfortunately, many theologians, teachers, preachers, and church members consider the glory of God to be a thing of the past: something that was known in biblical times, in events such as the deliverance of the Israelites from Egypt, but cannot be experienced today. Yet the glory of God is for our present generation. God desires to reveal His glory to His people and to the world, and He will do so through our lives as we seek Him. *"You will seek Me and find Me, when you search for Me with all your heart"* (Jeremiah 29:13). In this first study, we will begin our search by discovering what the Word of God says about our heavenly Father as the unparalleled, glorious God.

Study Questions

Part I: God's Glory Fills Heaven and Earth

1. What belongs to the Lord God? (1 Chronicles 29:11)

_____

_____

_____

2. What does the *"great multitude in heaven"* declare about God? (Revelation 19:1)

_____

_____

REFLECTIONS ON THE
BIBLICAL MEANING OF GLORY

A Hebrew word translated as *"glory"* in the Old Testament is *kabowd*. Its literal meaning is "weight," but it is used figuratively in the sense of "splendor," "abundance," "honor," or "glory"; it is something "glorious." *Kabowd* is used variously to describe an individual's wealth, power or majesty, influential position, or great honor. (See, for example, Genesis 31:1; 45:13.) *Kabowd* can also express fame, reputation, recognition, beauty, magnificence, strength, dignity, splendor, respect, excellence, holiness, and greatness. (See, for example, Exodus 28:2; Psalm 49:16–17.) From these connotations, we may conclude that the glory of God expresses all of His attributes.

A Greek word that best expresses the meaning of *kabowd* in the New Testament is *doxa*. It leads to the notion of reputation, honor, fame, praise, dignity, splendor, and brilliance. *Doxa* speaks of the real majesty belonging to God as the Supreme Governor—majesty in the sense of the absolute perfection of His deity.

<u>KEY DEFINITION</u>: The glory of God is the total sum of His attributes, character, and intrinsic virtues, the brilliance of His presence, and the splendor of His majesty.

3. Where did the psalmist say God has *"set"* His glory? (Psalm 8:1b)

_____

4. (a) What do the heavens declare? (Psalm 19:1a)

_____

(b) What does the firmament show? (Verse 1b)

_____

(c) What did the psalmist say about the ability of the heavens and earth to communicate God's glory to people throughout the world? (Psalm 19:3–4a)

_____

_____

_____

5. What else do the heavens declare? (Psalm 97:6a)

_____

6. The seraphim are special angels who dwell at God's throne. What do they say is full of God's glory? (Isaiah 6:3b)

_____

7. Is there anywhere we can go that God is not present? (Psalm 139:7–12)

_____

8. Like David, what should we make a point to meditate on? (Psalm 145:5)

_____

Part II: To God Be the Glory

9. What do the seraphim declare about God that reveals an essential aspect of His glory? (Isaiah 6:3a)

_____

*The glory (presence) of God is the spiritual atmosphere of heaven,
like air is the physical atmosphere of earth.*

10. What does God say concerning those who would try to usurp His glory, or attribute glory to something other than Him? (Isaiah 42:8b)

_____

_____

11. (a) What shouldn't the wise man glory in? (Jeremiah 9:23)

_____

(b) What shouldn't the mighty man glory in? (Verse 23)

_____

(c) What shouldn't the rich man glory in? (Verse 23)

_____

12. What should a person glory in? (Jeremiah 9:24a; 1 Corinthians 1:31)

_____

_____

13. Which works does the Lord delight in exercising? (Jeremiah 9:24b)

_____

_____

Only God has intrinsic glory: "He who glories, let him glory in the LORD."

Part III: God Shares His Glory

14. Considering God's greatness and glory, how do we know He is interested in what goes on in the world He created? (Psalm 113:5–6)

_____

_____

15. Although God will not allow anyone to usurp His glory, what does He desire to give to those who love Him and walk according to His ways? (Psalm 84:11b) Choose one of the following by circling the letter:

(a) grace

(b) glory

(c) every good thing

(d) all of the above

God desires to share His glory with His people.

---

16. What term for God did the apostle Paul use that combines the concepts of His love and His majesty? Complete the following:

Ephesians 1:17: "_...that the God of our Lord Jesus Christ, _____ _____

_____ _____, may give to you the spirit of wisdom and revelation in the

knowledge of Him._"

17. What is God's purpose for His "_sons_"—all those who have become His children through faith in Christ Jesus? Complete the following:

Hebrews 2:10: "_For it was fitting for [God], for whom are all things and by whom are

all things, in _____ _____ _____ _____

_____, to make the captain of their salvation [Jesus] perfect through

sufferings._"

18. In Jesus' prayer to God the Father shortly before His arrest and crucifixion, what did He affirm that He had given His followers? (John 17:22a)

_____

19. What has God given us as a *"guarantee,"* *"deposit"* (NIV), or down payment for the fullness of His glory? (2 Corinthians 5:5b)

_____

The glory of God is the essence of all that He is.

Conclusion

There are numerous aspects to God's glory, and He desires to show these dimensions of His glory to those who love and serve Him. In the glory of God—in His manifest presence—everything "is"; therefore, every need of humanity can be met, so that we are complete. In the glory are healing, deliverance, and miracles (even creative miracles, such as new organs being formed), as you will read about in the "Experiences with God's Glory" sections at the end of each study.

Many people do not understand God's glory because they have never experienced it, either personally or through a church or ministry. I pray that you will have supernatural experiences even as you progress through this Bible study. I consider of utmost importance the sections at the end of each study entitled "Prayer of Activation" and "Action Steps." Don't allow this course to be only an intellectual exercise for you. Use it as a guide to bring you into the very presence of God.

Prayer of Activation

Father of glory, thank You for revealing Your magnificence to the world and for making known to Your people, in a personal way, Your glory, holiness, and grace. Grant us a deep desire to know You in Your fullness and to receive all You desire to give us through Your glory. Release the riches of Your glory into our lives, even now, and let us live in Your presence. In the name of Jesus, amen.

Action Steps

- ◆ Meditate on the following Scriptures and incorporate them into your prayers and your worship of God: Ephesians 1:17–21; 1 Chronicles 29:11; Isaiah 6:3; Jeremiah 9:24.

- ◆ Each day this week, choose an aspect of creation and consider how it "declares" the glory of God. Then, offer praise and worship to God for His surpassing glory.

EXPERIENCES WITH GOD'S GLORY

Transformations, Miracles, and Healings

Some time ago, Pastor Guillermo Maldonado was invited to minister in Cochabamba, Bolivia, where approximately 3,500 pastors and leaders gathered together. On the last day of the meetings, the Holy Spirit led him to teach and guide the people to have an encounter with His glory. After the teaching, the presence of God manifested, and everyone began to cry out. Each person there was touched by the presence of God. Some people were crying out for forgiveness of their sins and asking God how to move in the supernatural, while others simply expressed that they wanted to serve Him. Everyone cried out according to the desire of his or her heart.

In the midst of this movement, God transformed the hearts of every leader present. The proof is that they took everything they received and shared it with their own congregations. Furthermore, miracles and amazing healings took place. A woman diagnosed with terminal cancer had been carried in on a stretcher. When she was exposed to the glory of God, she got up, completely healed! Another indigenous woman, who did not speak Spanish, had a type of rash. She had terrible boils that covered her entire face. This woman had already consulted all the witches and sorcerers in the region. She had desperately searched for a solution, but no one was able to heal her. Then, the presence of God fell upon her—without anyone touching her or translating anything we were saying—and, suddenly, every boil disappeared, and she received her healing. On the platform, she was yelling in Quechua, which is the dialect of her region, "Thank You, Daddy! What the witches and sorcerers were unable to do in years, You have done!" The weight of glory was so strong that the entire ministry team began to cry. The musicians fell under the weight of the presence of God. No one could stand. The 3,500 leaders gathered in that building were deeply impacted by His glory.

Study 2

YOU ARE MADE FOR GLORY

"Then God said, 'Let Us make man in Our image, according to Our likeness....'
So God created man in His own image; in the image of God He created him;
male and female He created them."
—Genesis 1:26–27

Introduction

When God created human beings, He bestowed His glory on them as a gift. And glory is the inheritance of every child of God—those whom Jesus Christ has redeemed from sin and death. We are specially designed for God's glory. As Jesus prayed,

> *And the glory which You* [God the Father] *gave Me I have given them, that they may be one just as We are one.* (John 17:22)

God's glory was the environment in which the first human beings lived before they rejected His loving command and were separated from His presence. For us to be disconnected from God's presence is spiritual and physical death. Yet, when we remain connected to His presence—when we, in essence, continually draw in His breath, the breath through which He gave life to Adam—we experience true life. *"Man shall not live by bread alone, but by every word that proceeds from the mouth of God"* (Matthew 4:4).

Study Questions

Part I: Life Within God's Glory

1. By whom were the heavens and earth made? (Genesis 1:1)

2. (a) Genesis 1:11–12 explains that God created vegetation on the earth. What did He cause to appear first as an environment in which that vegetation could live? (Genesis 1:9b–10a)

_____

(b) In Genesis 1:20a, we read that God created sea creatures. What did He prepare first as an environment in which those creatures could live? (Verses 9a, 10b)

_____

(c) Genesis 1:24–25 tells how God created animals. What did He produce first as an integral part of the environment that would nourish and sustain their lives? (Verse 11)

_____

_____

Before God created anything, He prepared the environment that would perfectly sustain it.

3. (a) From what did God form the man's (Adam's) body? (Genesis 2:7a)

_____

(b) What action did God take to cause the man to become a living being? (Verse 7b)

_____

(c) How did God create the woman (Eve)? (Verses 21–22a)

_____

4. In whose image were human beings—both male and female—created? (Genesis 1:26–27)

_____

5. What is God's essential being, as described by the apostle John? Complete the following:

   John 4:24: *"God is* _____*."*

6. What is the essence of a human being—something that is both greater than and separate from his physical body and that returns to God after the body dies? (Ecclesiastes 12:7)

   _____

7. Whom does God the Father seek to worship Him? (John 4:23b)

   _____

8. In Psalm 8, David praised God, mentioning several ways in which He has designed man to reflect His image and likeness. Complete the following:

   (a) Verse 5b: *"You have* _____ _____ _____

   _____ _____ _____*."*

   (b) Verse 6: *"You have* _____ _____ _____ _____

   _____ *over the works of Your hands; You have* _____

   _____ _____ _____ _____ _____*."*

The glory of an individual resides in his intrinsic worth.

---

9. (a) God prepared the special environment in which man was to live on earth. How was this act of preparation described? Complete the following:

   Genesis 2:8a: *"The LORD God* _____ _____

   _____ *eastward in Eden...."*

(b) What elements were included in that environment? (Genesis 2:9–10a)

_____

_____

_____

(c) How did Adam come to live in the garden? (Verse 8b)

_____

10. (a) Whose presence was in the garden with Adam and Eve? (Genesis 3:8a)

_____

(b) What was one way in which God's presence in the garden was perceived by Adam and Eve? Complete the following:

Verse 8a: "And [Adam and Eve] _____ _____ _____

_____ _____ _____ _____ *walking in the garden*…."

REFLECTIONS ON EDEN AS THE ENVIRONMENT OF GOD'S GLORY

In Hebrew, the word *"Eden"* means "pleasure" or "delight," while the word *"garden"* signifies "enclosure" or a "fenced" place. It comes from a root word meaning "to hedge about"; it is something that "protects," "defends," "covers," or "surrounds." When we are in God's glory, we are surrounded and protected by God's presence. I believe that, rather than being a particular geographical place, Eden was a carefully prepared, delightful "spot" of glory that God designed mankind to dwell in.

God put Adam right into the environment of His presence and glory. He never told Adam, "I want you to search for Eden." He placed him there. He didn't give him any choice because that was the only environment in which he could be sustained and thrive. And, in that setting, God revealed Himself and His ways to humanity.

KEY DEFINITION: Eden was a spot on the earth for a moment in time where the presence of God was a gate to heaven.

Part II: Life Outside God's Glory

11. What commandment did God give Adam (and, through him, to Eve) regarding his environment, including the consequence for violating it? (Genesis 2:16–17)

_____

_____

_____

12. (a) God's enemy, the devil, who had taken the form of a serpent, tempted the first human beings to violate God's command. (See Genesis 3:1–6) How did they respond? (Verse 6b)

_____

_____

(b) What were Eve's motivations for her actions? (Verse 6a)

_____

_____

13. (a) What had the serpent told Eve *would* and *would not* happen if she ate the fruit of the tree of the knowledge of good and evil? (Genesis 3:4–5)

_____

_____

(b) Were Adam and Eve already like God? If so, in what way? (Genesis 1:26a, 27a)

_____

(c) Did Adam and Eve die after eating the fruit of the tree of the knowledge of good and evil, just as God had said they would? (Genesis 5:5; Romans 5:12)

_____

14. (a) What was the immediate result for Adam and Eve after they ate the fruit of the tree? (Genesis 3:7a)

_____

(b) How did they react to this discovery? (Verse 7b)

_____

(c) How did Adam and Eve react to God's presence after they had disobeyed His command? (Verse 8b)

_____

The presence of God—His glory—is not a "place" but an environment.

---

15. In what state are human beings when they are separated from God? (Ephesians 2:1b)

_____

16. God told Adam and Eve of the various consequences and curses that would fall on them due to their willful act of disobedience. (See Genesis 3:16–19.) What other action did He take in regard to the environment in which Adam (and Eve) lived? Complete the following:

(a) Genesis 3:23a: "The Lord God _____ _____ [Adam and Eve] _____ _____ _____ _____ _____ _____ .…"

(b) Genesis 3:24: *"So He* _____ _____ _____
_____...."

17. What did God place at the east of the garden to guard the way to the tree of life, so that Adam and Eve could not return and eat of it in their present state? (Genesis 3:24b)

    _____

18. What has been the behavior and condition of all human beings since Adam and Eve's disobedience and exile from the garden of Eden? (Romans 3:23)

    _____

19. Thousands of years after Eden, the nation of Israel experienced a tragic loss when the ark of the covenant—the place where God chose to manifest His presence to His people—was captured by the Philistines. What statement did the daughter-in-law of Eli the priest make that also describes humanity's rejection of God in the garden and subsequent loss of His presence? (1 Samuel 4:21a)

    _____

Sin caused man to fall short of the glory of God and to be exiled from His presence.

---

20. God made a declaration to the serpent (the devil) that was the first of many promises He would make concerning the coming of the Messiah, the Redeemer of humanity. The Messiah would defeat the devil and restore human beings to their lost glory. What are the words of this first messianic promise? (Genesis 3:15)

    _____

    _____

REFLECTIONS ON LOST GLORY

God's presence is pure, uncontaminated, holy. Human beings did not essentially fall from a place; they fell from God's presence, from the environment of glory. So, humanity as a whole has been "short" of His glory from that day. Human beings' existence under the curse of sin is one of lost relationship with God and lost potential of life in His glory. Left to ourselves, we are unable to live in accordance with the high existence for which we were created.

When Adam and Eve sinned, their spirits—the essence of who they were as human beings made in the image of God—died. They also began to die physically. If something is removed from its natural environment, you don't have to actively kill it; it will die on its own. For example, if you take a fish out of water, it will slowly die of suffocation. Likewise, if you pull up a plant from the earth and set it on top of the ground, it will soon wither and die from lack of water and nutrients. In the case of Adam and Eve, they essentially removed themselves from God's presence by choosing to go against His ways and seeking to live outside the parameters of His glory and protection. Yet God created mankind to live in His glory— that was His plan from the beginning. This is the reason human beings die when they are estranged from His presence. It is the environment we were designed for! We are meant to have God's glory within us and to be surrounded by the glory of His presence.

That which is created cannot live independently of its God-given environment; it will die.

---

21. God desires human beings to be His own "garden," the place where His glory dwells and through which He accomplishes His purposes in the world. In the Old Testament, how are the *"house of Israel"* and the *"men of Judah"* depicted? (Isaiah 5:7a)

_____

_____

22. (a) In the New Testament, what did Jesus call Himself, using similar imagery? (John 15:1a)

_____

(b) What did He call the heavenly Father? (Verse 1b NIV)

_____

23. (a) What are we in relation to Jesus, the *"vine"*? (John 15:5a)

_____

(b) What will we produce if we abide in Jesus, and He in us, thereby enabling us to live in God's presence and glory? (John 15:5b)

_____

24. (a) What do the Scriptures say about those who are continually guided by God? Complete the following:

Isaiah 58:11b: *"You shall be like a* _____ _____,

and like a _____ _____ _____, *whose*

_____ _____ _____ _____*."*

(b) What statement did Jesus make about Himself as the Provider of this perpetual, flourishing life? (John 7:38)

_____

_____

The glory of God was the original environment in which mankind lived, and it is the environment to which we must return if we are to have abundant spiritual life.

Conclusion

Human beings' wonderful existence in God's glory—the atmosphere for which they were created—did not last. Adam and Eve sinned by choosing to rebel against God's instructions. As a result, they were disconnected from His life and were separated from the fullness of His glory. As we have seen, they fell *"short of the glory of God"* (Romans 3:23).

Adam and Eve lost the tangible presence of God when they disobeyed Him. It is sad when the presence of God departs, and it is pitiful today to observe believers, churches, and ministries that "survive" without it, having only an appearance of holiness and godliness. On the surface, everything may appear to be fine, but the truth is that the presence of God is not on the inside. When you see a church in which no one is getting saved; people are not changed or transformed; holiness is not encouraged; miracles, healing, and the power of

God are nonexistent; and God's presence is no longer evident, it means that place is without glory—and this is equivalent to death.

God is everywhere, all the time, but He doesn't manifest Himself tangibly everywhere on earth today. He manifests Himself where He is welcomed, where people are in right relationship with Him through Jesus Christ, and where they seek His glory. Eden was an environment that was a "gate" to heaven because God manifested His glory there to human beings who were made in His image and were in unbroken fellowship with Him. God's presence with humanity was truly heaven on earth. It is time for all of us to diligently seek the manifestation of His glory once more so that we may receive the very life of God and be transformed into His likeness. (See 2 Corinthians 3:17–18.)

Prayer of Activation

Father of glory, forgive us for the times when we have acted like Adam and Eve—going our own ways, living for ourselves, and not trusting You and Your Word. Pour out Your Spirit into our hearts now as we seek You and Your glory in our lives. Transform us into Your likeness, so that Your thoughts are our thoughts and Your ways are our ways. May we experience Your presence in a tangible way, for the earth is filled with Your glory. Then, activate us for Your service, through Your Spirit. In Jesus' name, amen.

Action Steps

+ Think about how you feel or react in God's presence when you know you have disobeyed Him or have neglected to do what He has asked you to do. Do you try to "hide" from Him, as Adam and Eve did? How successful were they at hiding from God? Read 1 John 1:8–9 to remind yourself of how He wants you to respond if you sin. Then, confess your sins and receive His loving forgiveness.

+ Commit the following passage to memory and say it every morning:

I am the vine, you are the branches. He who abides in Me, and I in him, bears much fruit; for without Me you can do nothing. If anyone does not abide in Me, he is cast out as a branch and is withered; and they gather them and throw them into the fire, and they are burned. If you abide in Me, and My words abide in you, you will ask what you desire, and it shall be done for you. By this My Father is glorified, that you bear much fruit; so you will be My disciples. (John 15:5–8)

EXPERIENCES WITH GOD'S GLORY

Deliverances from Addictions and Depression

Invited by a friend, we arrived at [King Jesus Ministry], devastated. Our son David had spent one day in jail because of a drug problem and bad behavior, and, because of this, he had lost his scholarship to Nova School of Medicine. When we arrived at the parking lot of the church, we suddenly felt a supernatural presence invade our car. My son began to cry and sob while asking God and us to forgive him. My wife began to cry and tremble. I was paralyzed and astonished. If this was happening in the parking lot, the first time we visited the church, then what was going to happen when we entered the church? About thirty minutes later, we were able to leave the car. As a result of our visit to the church, David was transformed. God delivered him and turned him into an evangelist to drug addicts, a House of Peace [the church's home fellowship ministry] leader, a member of the university evangelistic team, a warrior of intercession, and an example to many of his old friends. As for me, I had neglected my relationships with God and my family due to alcoholism. The Lord delivered me from this addiction, and I was reconciled to Him. God also began to restore my marriage. My wife, Joy, was delivered from depression and her dependency on antidepressants. This firsthand experience transformed our lives and gave us purpose. It gave new destiny to my family and my future generations.

Study 3

THE LORD OF GLORY CAME TO EARTH

"And without controversy great is the mystery of godliness: God was manifested in the flesh, justified in the Spirit, seen by angels, preached among the Gentiles, believed on in the world, received up in glory."
—1 Timothy 3:16

Introduction

Though mankind turned its back on its Creator, God was *"not willing that any should perish but that all should come to repentance"* (2 Peter 3:9). He provided a way for us to be restored to Him and His glory, implementing a plan of action to rescue us that included: (1) God the Son, Jesus Christ, coming to earth to be born as a human being and to live a completely sinless life; (2) Jesus dying in our place as our Substitute, taking our punishment for sin; (3) Jesus being raised from the dead and ascending to heaven, thereby conquering sin and death. With the shedding of His blood, Jesus redeemed us from sin and sickness; and, with His resurrection, He gave us access to eternity, bringing our spirits from death to life. God's glory is in us! Jesus' atoning blood gives us access to the Father and reconnects our spirits with His presence, while our bodies wait to be completely redeemed from death, as well. (See 1 Corinthians 15:42–45.)

The plan of salvation demonstrates that, even though mankind sinned, God's purpose will be carried out according to this cycle: the glory of God was present at the beginning of creation, and it will manifest powerfully in the last days—it will be seen in our time. The redeeming work of Jesus allows us to live once more according to God's glory in spirit, in soul (mind, will, and emotions), and, even to a large extent, in body. It may not be easy, but we will go *"from glory to glory"* (2 Corinthians 3:18) if we believe and persevere.

Study Questions

Part I: Jesus' Glory in Eternity

1. Shortly before Jesus' sacrificial death on the cross, with what glory did He ask the Father to glorify Him? (John 17:5b)

2. (a) When was Jesus foreordained in His divine mission to come to earth as a Man and to be the Redeemer of humanity? (1 Peter 1:20a)

    _____

    (b) At what point did Jesus come to earth to fulfill His mission, and for whom did He come? Complete the following:

    Verses 20b–21a: "…[He] *was manifest* _____ _____ _____

    _____ _____ _____ _____ _____

    _____ _____ _____ _____."

    (c) What did God do for Jesus after He had completed this mission? (Verse 21b)

    _____

3. With what title did the apostle Paul refer to Jesus, acknowledging His divine origin and glory? (1 Corinthians 2:8b)

    _____

REFLECTIONS ON
JESUS AS THE BRIGHTNESS OF GOD'S GLORY

When Jesus Christ came to earth to be our Savior, He was the ultimate expression of the manifestation of God's glory in the world. *"Who being the brightness of His glory and the express image of His person, and upholding all things by the word of His power, when He had by Himself purged our sins, sat down at the right hand of the Majesty on high"* (Hebrews 1:3).

Jesus made the following statements: *"I and My Father are one"* (John 10:30). *"The Father is in Me and I in Him"* (John 10:38). *"He who has seen Me has seen the Father.…The Father who dwells in Me does the works"* (John 14:9–10). Jesus led us to know the Father through His character, virtues, and behavior. To see Him was to see the splendor and image of the Father. His substance (essence) was His glory, and to hear Him was the same as hearing the Father.

<u>KEY DEFINITION</u>: When referring to Jesus, the Greek word *doxa* in the New Testament, which means "glory," alludes to the majestic royalty of the Messiah—this being

the highest level of exaltation and the condition to which the Father raised Jesus after He had fulfilled His purpose on earth, defeating Satan and death.

Part II: Jesus' Glory on Earth

4. (a) What did Jesus' birth as a human being bring to God, as the angels expressed after announcing the birth to the shepherds? Complete the following:

   Luke 2:14a: "_____ to God in the highest...."

   (b) What did Jesus' birth bring to men?

   Verse 14b: "...and on earth _____, _____

   toward men!"

5. In what way did Luke describe the works of Jesus, such as healing and delivering people from Satan's oppression? Complete the following:

   Luke 13:17b: "...and all the multitude rejoiced for all the _____

   things that were done by Him."

6. What did Jesus receive from God the Father when He was transfigured before His disciples Peter, James, and John (see Matthew 17:1–9; Luke 9:28–36)? (2 Peter 1:17a)

   _____

7. What did the people proclaim when Jesus made His triumphal entrance into Jerusalem, an event we now commemorate on Palm Sunday? (Luke 19:38)

   _____

   _____

8. What did Jesus say about Himself shortly before His crucifixion? (John 13:31)

   _____

9. Why did Jesus ask the Father to glorify Him? (John 17:1b) Choose one of the following by circling the letter:

   (a) so He could feel good about Himself

   (b) to prove that He was better than those around Him

   (c) so He could glorify the Father

   (d) so He could escape crucifixion

The temptation to prove yourself
is not a valid reason to manifest the power and glory of God.

---

10. (a) What had Jesus accomplished for the Father through His ministry? (John 17:4a)

    _____

    (b) In what way did He do this? (Verse 4b)

    _____

Part III: Jesus' Glory Given to Men

11. What was Jesus crowned with for suffering and dying for us? (Hebrews 2:9)

    _____

12. What happened to Jesus after He was resurrected from the dead? Complete the following:

    1 Timothy 3:16: "*God was manifested in the flesh,...believed on in the world,*

    _____ _____ _____ _____."

13. (a) Before Jesus ascended to heaven, what authority had the Father given Him, and for what purpose had He given it? (John 17:2)

    _____

    _____

(b) What is eternal life? (John 17:3)

_____

_____

---
*Jesus is the highest expression of God to mankind,
the complete revelation and manifestation of the glory of the Father.*

---

14. (a) Recall the specific glory Jesus has given His followers. (John 17:22a)

_____

(b) What does Jesus desire for all whom the Father has given Him? (Verse 24a)

_____

_____

15. What did Christ become for us when we received Him? Complete the following:

1 Corinthians 1:30: *"Christ Jesus…became for us* _____

_____ _____ *; and* _____ *and*

_____ *and* _____ *."*

16. For whose glory did God ordain the *"hidden wisdom"* that He revealed in Christ? (1 Corinthians 2:7b)

_____

17. In a previous lesson, we learned that when God made the captain of their salvation (Jesus) perfect through sufferings, He was doing something specific for His *"many sons."* What was He doing? (Hebrews 2:10)

_____

REFLECTIONS ON RECLAIMED GLORY

At the cross, Jesus became the recipient of all the sins committed by humanity. He became like every other human being—carrying our iniquity and rebellion. Though He was born without sin and never sinned, He became sin of His own free will because of His love for us, in order to conform to our nature, so that we could *"become the righteousness of God in Him"* (2 Corinthians 5:21). He left His heavenly glory behind to reach us in our fallen nature. Yet, when He was resurrected, He reclaimed His glory and then gave it back to His people so they could be transformed and shaped according to the glory of the Father.

Jesus conformed to our image so we could be transformed into His likeness.

---

18. For what reason has God, who commanded light to shine out of darkness, shone in our hearts? (2 Corinthians 4:6b)

    _____

    _____

19. What should we desire for others to experience, in the same way we have? Complete the following:

    2 Corinthians 4:4b: "…[that] *the light of the gospel of the glory of Christ, who is the image of God,* _____ _____ _____ _____."

20. What statement did Paul write in his second letter to the Corinthians, emphasizing that it is the glory of God living within His people that does the work, and not themselves? (2 Corinthians 4:7)

    _____

    _____

21. What comparable statement from the Old Testament did Paul quote in his first letter to the Corinthians? (1 Corinthians 1:31)

_____

22. What is *"the hope of glory"*? (Colossians 1:27b)

_____

23. As the Ephesians' understanding was enlightened by the spirit of wisdom and revelation in the knowledge of God, what did Paul want them to know? (Ephesians 1:18b–19a)

_____

_____

_____

Conclusion

God the Son set aside His rightful glory in heaven to come to earth as a Man, only to receive that glory again as He obeyed the Father, did miracles and other works in the Father's name, and fulfilled His earthly mission. Jesus did this so that, in a parallel way, the glory we had been given in creation—and subsequently lost—might be returned to us as we live in Him and He in us.

In Christ, we are all carriers of a "portable Eden"; wherever we go, we carry with us His glory through the indwelling Holy Spirit. We have access to our original environment—God's presence—through the blood of Jesus. When we return to our true environment, we have true life. Jesus said, *"I am the way, the truth, and the life"* (John 14:6), and *"He who abides in Me, and I in him, bears much fruit; for without Me you can do nothing"* (John 15:5).

Remember, you are *made* for glory—for existing continually in God's presence as you live your life. Although the Holy Spirit already dwells within believers, we need to actively seek God and His glory through worship, praise, surrender to His will, and faith. Why? Jesus said, *"The spirit indeed is willing, but the flesh is weak"* (Matthew 26:41; Mark 14:38). Until the day when we will once again live in uninterrupted glory, we must seek God's glory daily!

Prayer of Activation

Father of glory, we praise You that, through Jesus, we live in Your presence and walk once more according to Your glory. Let our whole lives glorify you, just as Jesus' did, as we complete the work You have given us to do on earth. To have eternal life is to know You as the true God, and to know Jesus Christ, whom You have sent. Jesus is our wisdom, our righteousness, our sanctification, and our redemption. Impart to us the light of the knowledge of the glory of God in the face of Jesus Christ. Be glorified in us, O Lord. Let us see Your glory. We say, as the angels said, "Glory to God in the highest!" Amen!

Action Steps

+ Ask God to enlighten the eyes of your understanding, so that you will know the hope of His calling, the riches of the glory of His inheritance in the saints, and the exceeding greatness of His power toward you. (See Ephesians 1:18–19.)

+ Pray for several people today whom you know need Jesus, asking the Father to soften their hearts, so that they may receive the light of the gospel of the glory of Christ through the ministry of the Holy Spirit. Then, ask God to create an opportunity for you to share the gospel with them, and trust Him to reveal Himself to them.

EXPERIENCES WITH GOD'S GLORY

Miraculous Healing of AIDS

In Medellín, Colombia, there is a woman named Johanna who works with institutions for children who are orphaned, homeless, and infected with AIDS. A year ago, she accepted Jesus as her Lord and Savior when she visited King Jesus Ministry. There, she was trained to move in the supernatural power of God. When she returned to Colombia and to the orphanage where she works, she met Xiomara—a four-month-old girl who was diagnosed as HIV-positive. The love of God came upon Johanna, so she began to pray for the little girl, breaking the curse that had come upon her through her bloodline. When she did, she felt the power of God and knew that He had done something supernatural. Weeks later, after a series of exams, Xiomara was declared totally healed and was placed for adoption. Johanna witnessed the miracle take place before her eyes, and today, that little girl lives in a wonderful home with loving parents. Something similar happened to

Laura, a two-year-old girl who had been abandoned by her mother—a sixteen-year-old prostitute. The doctors had declared there was no hope for her recovery, but Johanna prayed for her, also, and the power of God created a miracle by restoring her immune system and eradicating the viral infection. The last three times she was examined, the results came back negative. She was declared healthy by the doctors and was placed for adoption.

Study 4

THE MANIFEST PRESENCE OF GOD

"Who is like You, O LORD, among the gods? Who is like You, glorious in holiness, fearful in praises, doing wonders?"
—Exodus 15:11

Introduction

God's glory is the realm of eternity. It is infinite, boundless, with no restrictions—it is beyond the imagination of human beings. God's *manifested* glory is eternity revealed on earth. It is the impact of His powerful and unforgettable mark, seen and heard in the natural world.

In the Old Testament, we see the glory of God manifested among the Israelites, and, in the New Testament, we see His glory manifested among Jewish and Gentile believers in His Son Jesus Christ. God's people experienced the manifestation of the glory in close proximity. It often appeared in the form of a cloud, known as the *shekinah*. *Shekinah* is a Hebrew word that refers to the "dwelling place of God" or "place where God rests"; it describes the eminent presence of God that transcends the spiritual realm and manifests in the physical world. *Shekinah* is related to the immediate and intimate activity of God—the splendor of the Lord while He is present in the now, in action, allowing others to know Him.

God will sometimes reveal His *shekinah* glory to human beings through physical phenomena, such as fire or clouds. At other times, He will reveal His *kabowd*, or *doxa*, glory—an aspect of His nature, attributes, and infinite perfection. In His sovereignty, He takes the initiative and decides which aspect of Himself to reveal. Of one thing we can be sure: the will of God has always been to dwell among His people and to manifest Himself to humanity.

In this study, we will review some examples from the Old and New Testaments in which God's presence was revealed to human beings.

Part I: Manifestations in the Old Testament

1. In giving a brief history of the nation of Israel, how did Stephen describe the calling of the patriarch Abraham, who is the father of all who believe? Complete the following:

    Acts 7:2–3: "…listen: _____ _____ _____ _____

    _____ _____ _____ _____

    _____…and said to him, 'Get out of your country and from your

    relatives, and come to a land that I will show you.'"

2. (a) How did God reveal His presence to Moses in a tangible way to get his attention in order to call him to a special task? (Exodus 3:2)

    _____

    _____

    (b) To what task was God commissioning Moses? (Verse 10)

    _____

3. (a) In what dual form did God reveal His *shekinah* glory, or His manifest presence, to the Israelites during their forty years in the desert? (Exodus 13:21)

    _____

    (b) Besides being a reminder that God was always with His people, what practical purpose did these manifestations provide? (Verse 21)

    _____

    _____

(c) What happened after Moses completed the tabernacle, which was the place of worship for the Israelites? (Exodus 40:34)

_____

_____

(d) How did the Israelites respond to the pillar of cloud and pillar of fire as they followed the Lord's leading in their journeys? (Verses 36–37)

_____

_____

4. What was the function of the cloud, as described by the psalmist? (Psalm 105:39a)

_____

KEY DEFINITION: A manifestation is a supernatural demonstration that can be perceived by the human senses.

5. (a) What physical manifestations took place when God revealed Himself to the Israelites shortly before He gave them the Law through Moses? (Exodus 19:16)

_____

_____

(b) Describe the appearance of Mt. Sinai. What was the reason it looked that way? (Verse 18)

_____

_____

(c) In what way did God answer after Moses spoke? (Exodus 19:19b)

_____

6. Describe what Moses and the leaders and elders of Israel saw when God revealed Himself to them. (Exodus 24:10b)

_____

_____

7. (a) From where did God speak to Moses in the tabernacle? (Exodus 25:22a; Numbers 7:89)

_____

(b) Where did the psalmist say God dwells? (Psalm 80:1)

_____

8. (a) What request did Moses make of God? (Exodus 33:18)

_____

(b) What did God tell Moses he could and could not experience of Him? (Verses 19a, 23)

_____

_____

9. What did Moses' face look like after he had been in the Lord's presence and had spoken with Him? (Exodus 34:29b–30)

_____

KEY DEFINITION: In His *sovereignty*, as demonstrated through manifestations of His glory, God does what He wants, when He wants, and in the way He wants, without bringing in the participation of human beings. It is God doing His own works.

10. (a) How did God make His presence known when Solomon commenced the dedication of the new temple in Jerusalem? (2 Chronicles 5:13b–14)

_____

_____

(b) What manifestations occurred after Solomon finished his prayer to the Lord? (2 Chronicles 7:1)

_____

_____

(c) How did Solomon and the other Israelites respond to these manifestations? (Verses 3–4)

_____

_____

11. (a) What physical phenomena were seen and heard by the prophet Elijah on the mountain, before he heard the Lord's voice as He was passing by? (1 Kings 19:11b–12a)

_____

_____

(b) Was the Lord "*in*" these particular manifestations at that time? (Verses 11b–12a)

_____

(c) In what specific form did Elijah hear God speak, following the fire? (Verse 12b)

_____

(d) What action did Elijah take to cover himself when he knew he was in the presence of the Lord? (1 Kings 19:13a)

_____

_____

When God speaks to us, He might do so in an audible voice,
or He might speak to our hearts.

_____

12.   In what way did the Lord manifest His glory and receive the prophet Elijah to heaven without his experiencing death? (2 Kings 2:11b)

_____

_____

13.   (a) Describe what the prophet Isaiah first saw in his vision of the Lord sitting on His heavenly throne. (Isaiah 6:1)

_____

(b) What were standing above the throne? (Verse 2)

_____

(c) What were they calling to one another? (Verse 3)

_____

_____

(d) What two things happened after they cried out? (Verse 4)

_____

14.   (a) What did Isaiah say after seeing this vision? (Isaiah 6:5)

_____

_____

(b) How was Isaiah able to stand in God's presence, even though he was sinful? (Isaiah 6:6–7)

_____

_____

_____

(c) What did the Lord say immediately after Isaiah's sin was cleansed, and how did Isaiah respond? (Verse 8)

_____

_____

15. (a) The prophet Ezekiel also had a vision of God on His throne, manifesting His glory. To what jewel did he compare the appearance of the *"likeness of a throne"*? (Ezekiel 1:26a)

_____

(b) What did Ezekiel see on the likeness of the throne, *"high above it"*? (Verse 26b)

_____

(c) How did he describe the appearance of the *"man"*? (Verses 27–28a)

_____

_____

_____

16. (a) How did Ezekiel explain this appearance? Complete the following:

Ezekiel 1:28: *"This was the appearance of* _____ _____ _____

_____ _____ _____ _____ _____."

(b) What did Ezekiel do when he saw this vision, and what did he hear? (Ezekiel 1:28b)

_____

(c) What was the Lord's purpose in speaking to him? (Ezekiel 2:3–4)

_____

_____

17. What audible manifestations of God's glory did the prophet Ezekiel hear after the Spirit lifted him up? (Ezekiel 3:12–13)

_____

_____

_____

God is everywhere, but He does not manifest His presence everywhere.

Part II: Manifestations in the New Testament

18. In what way did the shepherds experience God's glory when the angel of the Lord appeared and stood before them to tell them that Jesus the Savior had been born? (Luke 2:9b)

_____

19. (a) What did Jesus see and hear after He was baptized? (Matthew 3:16b–17)

_____

_____

(b) What detail did the gospel of Luke include about the manner in which the Holy Spirit descended like a dove? (Luke 3:22a)

_____

20. (a) Combining the descriptions from two gospel accounts, how did Jesus' appearance change as He prayed on the mountain, accompanied by Peter, James, and John, and was *"transfigured"*? (Luke 9:29; Matthew 17:2b)

_____

_____

(b) Some biblical scholars believe the gospel of Mark is based on the apostle Peter's recollections. What vivid words did Mark (perhaps from Peter's account) use to describe how Jesus' clothes changed? (Mark 9:3)

_____

(c) During the transfiguration, what Old Testament figures talked with Jesus about His impending crucifixion? (Luke 9:30)

_____

(d) In what way are they described as appearing? (Verse 31a)

_____

(e) In what way did God the Father manifest Himself to Peter, James, and John at the transfiguration, and what did He tell them? (Matthew 17:5)

_____

_____

_____

REFLECTIONS ON JESUS' TRANSFIGURATION

Why was Jesus transfigured? What was the purpose of His changing in this way, since He was perfect? Jesus had laid aside His glory before He came to this world to be a human being. Therefore, He experienced the same temptations that any of us experience. He had a physical body, and His human nature was able to sin. Otherwise, the temptations He endured would have been meaningless. Prior to His transfiguration, Jesus had operated under the anointing of the Holy Spirit, but, through this manifestation, God showed to three of His disciples Jesus' glory—the same glory that was available to them. When Jesus was transfigured, they were able to see Moses and Elijah with Him. I believe that Moses represents the Torah (the law) or the *logos* (the written Word of God); Elijah represents the church, God's power, and the *rhema* word (a word from God that speaks to our present circumstances and is in accordance with the Scriptures); the cloud represents the glory; and Jesus represents the kingdom of God, as well as both the former glory and—through His forthcoming resurrection—the latter glory.

In essence, God revealed to these three disciples that Jesus would bring His kingdom, His power, and His glory. Otherwise, how would the disciples have known that the two figures standing next to Jesus were Moses and Elijah? In the presence of God, people are known as they are. At the moment of Jesus' transfiguration, the disciples were able to see who Jesus was on the inside in a physical, visible, and tangible way.

21. (a) What manifestations were evident as God poured out His Holy Spirit on the followers of Jesus on the day of Pentecost? (Acts 2:2–3)

_____

_____

_____

(b) What ability did Jesus' followers receive when they were filled with the Holy Spirit? (Verse 4b)

_____

(c) What did the devout Jewish men who were visiting Jerusalem from a number of foreign nations say they heard the disciples speaking in their own languages? (Acts 2:11b)

_____

22. (a) What manifestation did Stephen see during his defense before the council when he looked into heaven? (Acts 7:55b)

_____

(b) What was Stephen's spiritual condition before he saw this sight? Complete the following:

Verse 55a: "But he, _____ _____ _____ _____

_____ _____...."

23. (a) In what manner did Saul (later called Paul) experience the glory of Jesus on the road to Damascus as he was traveling to persecute the Christians there? (Acts 9:3b–4)

_____

_____

_____

(b) What temporary physical effect did this experience have on Saul? (Verses 8a, 9a)

_____

(c) What occurred immediately after Ananias, one of Jesus' followers, placed his hands on Saul? (Verse 18a)

_____

(d) What had Ananias told Saul would happen to him at the same time he received his sight? (Acts 9:17b)

_____

(e) After Saul received his sight, what did he do? (Verse 18b)

_____

(f) Jesus had manifested Himself to Saul in order to call him to a special purpose. What was that purpose, which the Lord related to Ananias? (Verse 15)

_____

_____

In the glory of God, every need is met.

---

24. (a) While Paul and Silas were praying and singing hymns to God at midnight after being wrongfully beaten and imprisoned, what manifestation from God suddenly occurred, revealing His presence and power on their behalf? (Acts 16:26)

_____

_____

(b) In what ways did the jailer and his family respond to the witness of Paul and Silas after the jailer felt and saw these powerful signs from God? (Verses 33b, 34b)

_____

25. When John was confined to the island of Patmos, he was in the Spirit on the Lord's Day and received the *"Revelation of Jesus Christ"* (Revelation 1:1), in which the resurrected Jesus was depicted in His glory in symbolic form.

(a) How was Jesus clothed, and what was the appearance of His head, hair, eyes, and feet? (Revelation 1:13b–15a)

_____

_____

(b) To what did John compare Jesus' voice? (Verse 15b)

_____

(c) What did He have in His right hand, and what came out of His mouth? (Verse 16a)

_____

(d) How was His countenance described? (Verse 16b)

_____

(e) Further on in the vision, what occurred in the *"temple of the tabernacle of the testimony in heaven"* (Revelation 15:5) that was reminiscent of what happened when Moses completed the tabernacle and Solomon dedicated the temple? (Revelation 15:8a)

_____

There are dimensions of the glory of God that few humans can stand.

Conclusion

Moses knew that the glory of God was more than a theological concept. That is why he asked God to *show* him His glory—the most intimate aspect of His nature. The kingdom, the power, and the glory of God are heavenly realities that every believer can experience now.

Are you experiencing the glory of God in your life? You need to have a revelation of the reality of God's glory so you can see its manifestation. Then, as you encounter the presence of God, you will be changed, transformed, and ignited by spiritual passion.

As I wrote in the introduction to this Bible study, mere "religion" will never produce a supernatural experience with God because it is void of the glory and life of the Lord. Since the distinction between religion and God's glory is so crucial, in the next study, we will learn how religious attitudes hinder the manifestation of God's presence and how you can move beyond practicing religion to having an encounter with your heavenly Father. Don't stay in the same place—there's more for you in God than what you are now experiencing!

Prayer of Activation

Father of glory, we ask for a revelation of Your majesty so that we may know You in a deeper way. Impart to us the same earnest desire to know You that Abraham and Moses had. Show us manifestations of Your glory, and then activate us to make known Your glory to everyone around us. In Jesus' name, amen.

Action Steps

+ Have you witnessed any manifestations of the *shekinah* glory of God? If so, write down a description of these encounters with God's presence and glory, whether you have experienced them on your own or with other believers. Express gratitude to God for revealing Himself to you, and ask Him to continue doing so. Then, share your experiences of God's glory with others, so they may desire to experience His presence, also.

+ Take a step of faith and ask God to work through you to manifest His glory in the world. Pray that He will guide you in reaching out to your family members and friends to minister salvation, healings, and miracles. Then, following the leading of the Holy Spirit.

EXPERIENCES WITH GOD'S GLORY

A Creative Miracle of a New Kidney

Pastor Guillermo Maldonado was preaching in a series of meetings in Rosario, Argentina. On the last day of these meetings, while he was ministering to more than 3,500 leaders from all over the country, a manifestation of "fire" descended on the auditorium. The *shekinah* glory "burned" those who were present. Thousands were crying out to

God. While this was occurring, a young woman came to the altar to testify. She had been born without a left kidney due to a generational curse that had come from her grandfather to her mother and, finally, to her. To make matters worse, she had required surgery to restore minimum use of her right kidney. Because of her condition, she had been able to go to the bathroom only once or twice a day, even when she drank large quantities of liquids.

The fire of the glory—God's presence—had descended on the first night of the meetings, and this young woman had received her miracle then. Intense heat had traveled throughout the left side of her body, making its greatest impact in the kidney area. That night, she'd had to use the bathroom over ten times. The next day, after she was tested, her doctor confirmed that she had a left kidney and that the right one was working perfectly. This was a creative miracle! The indisputable proof that she had two healthy kidneys was her countless trips to the bathroom. Shocked at her miracle, she came forward, crying, and testified on that final night of meetings. Everyone could see her overwhelming emotion and utter joy. The presence of God was all over her. God had delivered her from the curse and completely healed her.

Study 5

NATURAL KNOWLEDGE AND REVEALED KNOWLEDGE

"For to be carnally minded is death, but to be spiritually minded is life and peace."
—Romans 8:6

Introduction

God reveals His glory to us through revelation—spiritual "vision," knowledge, and understanding. Receiving revelation from God is an essential step to living perpetually in the glory of His presence. *"For in Him we live and move and have our being"* (Acts 17:28). To understand what revelation is, so that we may receive it, we need to recognize that there are two types of knowledge: (1) knowledge that comes through our physical senses—mental, sensorial, or natural knowledge, and (2) knowledge (and wisdom) that comes directly from God—revealed knowledge, or spiritual revelation.

The first type of knowledge is scientific, theoretic, and practical. It is experienced through our five senses—sight, hearing, touch, smell, and taste. It is information or storable data acquired from and implemented in the natural world. Mental, sensorial, or natural knowledge must be sought after—an act that demands academic learning and discipline. People who live according to this type of knowledge often believe only in what their senses detect, nothing more.

Yet one cannot know God and His glory through sensorial information alone—even though such information is vital for living in the natural dimension of earth. God created the earthly dimension, and He manifests Himself in it, although He does not belong to it. He is beyond it. We must learn to distinguish between the two types of knowledge and receive revealed knowledge from God. To help us do so, in this study, we will take an overview of what the Bible says about these two realms of knowledge and what they teach us about God.

Study Questions

Part I: Helpful Lessons from the Natural World

Even though we live in a fallen world, God uses our physical environment on earth and aspects of our daily lives to reveal Himself and His truths. In the following questions, we will explore various examples of this type of revelation from God.

1. Lesson #1: God reveals His majesty through the created world.

   (a) As a review from study 1, what do the heavens declare? (Psalm 19:1a)

   _____

   (b) How widespread is their communication? (Verse 4)

   _____

   (c) What can human beings "see" from the created world? (Romans 1:20a)

   _____

   (d) What are those attributes? (Verse 20b)

   _____

2. Lesson #2: God demonstrates wisdom for our lives through the traits of various animals, which He created to live in our physical world.

   (a) What should a lazy person—and anyone else who wants to gain wisdom—observe about the ways of the ant? (Proverbs 6:6–8)

   _____

   _____

   (b) If we do not exercise diligence in providing for our basic needs, as illustrated by the ant—if we sleep when we should be working, for example (see Proverbs 6:10)—what may happen to us? (Verse 11)

   _____

3. Lesson #3: God uses the natural development and qualities of plant species, as well as the process of cultivation, to teach eternal spiritual principles.

   (a) What qualities and effects did Jesus note about a mustard seed that is sown into the ground, in comparing it with the kingdom of God? (Mark 4:31b–32)

   _____

   _____

   _____

   (b) Using the illustration of planting and harvesting a crop, what did the apostle Paul say a person will reap? (Galatians 6:7b)

   _____

   (c) What will we reap if we sow to the flesh, and what will we reap if we sow to the Spirit? (Verse 8)

   _____

4. Lesson #4: God uses analogies related to human skills and endeavors to teach people about their relationship with Him.

   (a) What did the Lord tell the prophet Jeremiah he needed to do before hearing His words? (Jeremiah 18:2a)

   _____

   (b) Describe what Jeremiah observed at the potter's house. (Verses 3–4)

   _____

   _____

   (c) What was the spiritual meaning of this illustration? Complete the following:

   Verse 6b: "…as the _____ is in the _____ _____, so are _____ _____ _____ _____, O house of Israel!"

Reason, common sense, and logic serve the soul as revelation serves the spirit.

5. Lesson #5: God discusses proverbial sayings and common human experiences with people to get them to think about spiritual realities.

(a) Jesus referred to a saying that farmers quoted after they'd planted the seed for their crops. What was that saying? (John 4:35a)

_____

(b) In relation to this saying, what new spiritual reality did Jesus want His disciples to recognize, which He stated, beginning with the words *"Behold, I say to you…"*? (Verse 35b)

_____

(c) What did Jesus say about the weather as He addressed the multitudes? (Luke 12:54–55 NIV)

_____

_____

_____

(d) What point did Jesus make to the multitudes as a follow-up to these sayings, in order to warn them of their carelessness about spiritual matters? (Verse 56 NIV)

_____

_____

Part II: Limitations of Natural Knowledge

As we have seen, aspects of the natural world, such as the functions of plants and animals, are instructive and helpful for gaining wisdom. However, natural knowledge can take us only so far, especially when it is influenced by the fallen nature. We must receive God's revelation in various forms—through His Word, His Spirit, His gifts, and other spiritual phenomena—to understand deeper spiritual reality, so that we may know God and His glory and manifest Him to the world.

6. (a) To review, what action did Adam and Eve take, believing it would enable them to expand their knowledge of divine things—an action that involved disobeying God's command? (Genesis 3:6)

    _____

    (b) While they must have sensed their spiritual failure and loss, what knowledge did they immediately gain? (Verse 7a)

    _____

    (c) What type of knowledge was it—knowledge of the physical realm or of the spiritual realm? (Verse 7a)

    _____

7. (a) What statement did Jesus make to Nicodemus that emphasizes there is a significant distinction between the natural and spiritual realms? (John 3:6)

    _____

    (b) Of what two entities must we be "*born again*" (John 3:3) in order to both see and enter the kingdom of God? (John 3:5)

    _____

8. (a) Can the physical senses of seeing and hearing, or even man's natural intellect or imagination, know what God has in mind for those who love Him? (1 Corinthians 2:9)

    _____

    (b) By what means do human beings gain such knowledge? (Verse 10a)

    _____

(c) What have believers received, and what have they *not* received, in order to know what God has freely given to them? (1 Corinthians 2:12a)

REFLECTIONS ON THE MIND OF FALLEN HUMANITY

When Adam and Eve disobeyed God, they essentially decided to rely on natural knowledge more than spiritual knowledge by eating of the tree of the knowledge of good and evil. As a result of their sin, their spirits died. Moreover, they went from having both kinds of knowledge—natural and revealed—to having only natural knowledge, that is, mental and sensorial knowledge. Sin destroyed their connection to their spiritual Source and to spiritual knowledge. From that moment, they began to consider everything from the perspective of natural knowledge. If you base your life on natural knowledge alone, what you perceive is only a shadow of what truly is. Your vision has become distorted.

A lack of revealed knowledge is a characteristic of spiritual death because we do not live according to spiritual reality. Anytime we try to trust in natural knowledge to operate in the supernatural, we are essentially eating of the tree of the knowledge of good and evil. Natural knowledge offers information, such as facts or data, but it does not have the ability to effect lasting transformation because it comes from the fallen mind of man, not from the mind of God. Revealed knowledge supersedes every rational analysis and carries with it the intrinsic power to transform.

Part III: Consequences of a Lack of Revealed Knowledge

9. What was the ultimate consequence for Adam and Eve after they disobeyed God and were cut off from their spiritual Source? (Genesis 3:19b; Romans 6:23a)

---

10. Contrast what it means to be carnally minded (having the mind-set of the fallen nature) and what it means to be spiritually minded. (Romans 8:6)

Adam and Eve exchanged spiritual, revealed knowledge for sensorial knowledge.

11. (a) What did the Lord say Israel had done in rejecting Him and worshipping man-made idols instead? Complete the following:

Jeremiah 2:11b: *"My people have* _____ _____

_____ _____ _____ _____ _____

_____*."*

(b) The people committed two evils in making this change. Their first evil was forsaking God. In doing so, what *"fountain"* did they lose? (Verse 13a)

_____

(c) The second evil was that they hewed cisterns for themselves, instead of receiving water from God's fountain. What were the only kind of cisterns they were they capable of building? (Verse 13b)

_____

12. In question 1 of study 5, we learned that God's invisible attributes may be recognized and understood through the world He has created.

(a) What can happen to people when they reject the revealed knowledge of God and refuse to glorify and thank Him? (Romans 1:21b)

_____

(b) When people profess to be wise based only on their carnal knowledge, into what image of worship do they change the glory of the incorruptible God? (Verse 23b)

_____

_____

(c) For what do they exchange the truth of God? (Romans 1:25a)

_____

(d) When people do not want to retain God in their knowledge, what kind of mind might He give them over to? (Verse 28a)

_____

(e) What else might God give them up to, and what does this lead to? (Verse 24)

_____

_____

13. What predicament were the Israelites in at the time Samuel the prophet was born, a problem that indicated their spiritual poverty? (1 Samuel 3:1b)

_____

14. In the following Bible translations of Proverbs 29:18, what happens to people who have no revelation (*"vision"* KJV), or revealed knowledge, from God?

(a) NKJV, NIV: _____

(b) KJV: _____

15. What similar idea was conveyed by God through the prophet Hosea? (Hosea 4:6a)

_____

The enemy will destroy you in any area where you lack knowledge.

REFLECTIONS ON
BIBLICAL WORDS FOR "REVELATION"

The Hebrew word that is translated *"revelation,"* *"vision,"* or a comparable word in Proverbs 29:18, depending on the Bible version, is *chazown.* This word can also mean "oracle" or "divine communication." *Chazown* refers to a fresh revelation from God that declares what He is saying and doing now. Different from biblical doctrine or knowledge gained from reading the Scriptures or hearing Bible teachings, this communication is *rhema,* a "now" word from God. It is the manna that God provides for today—not for yesterday or for tomorrow. There will be another fresh revelation tomorrow that will keep us moving forward so that we don't lose our direction or advancement. This is the revelation of the Holy Spirit. Without *chazown,* the people *"cast off restraint"* (NKJV, NIV), they are *"uncontrolled"* (NCV), they are *"demoralized"* (NAB), they *"perish"* (KJV). They are lost, lacking destiny. What does this mean for us? We are currently living in times of darkness, confusion, and insecurity. Now, more than ever, we need God's fresh revelation.

In the New Testament, the word *"revelation"* is translated from the Greek word *apokalypsis,* which means to "reveal," "remove the covering," "discover," or "manifest something that was hidden." Revealed knowledge comes directly or indirectly from God's Holy Spirit to the spirit of a person, not to the person's mind or senses. Again, it cannot be researched in a book or in any other source of information. And it does not require time to learn, because it is given instantly; it manifests in the blink of an eye.

Part IV: Man's Knowledge Versus God's Knowledge

Even those who love God and desire to live for Him can still have a tendency to rely too much on natural knowledge, rather than walk in the light of His revealed knowledge. We don't need to have rejected the knowledge of God to experience some of the consequences of a lack of revealed knowledge. Let us therefore continue to explore what the Bible says about natural knowledge versus spiritual knowledge.

16. (a) What does the book of Proverbs warn us not to do? (Proverbs 3:5b, 7a)

_____

_____

(b) In contrast, what are we encouraged to do? (Proverbs 3:5a, 6a)

_____

_____

(c) What will the Lord do for us if we follow His instructions? (Verse 6b)

_____

17. Why do we need to be careful about following a path that seems right to us, from a natural or carnal point of view, while ignoring God's ways? (Proverbs 14:12b)

_____

18. (a) How did the apostle Paul describe the wisdom of this world? Complete the following:

1 Corinthians 3:19a: *"The wisdom of this world is* _____

_____ _____.*"*

(b) What does the Lord know about the thoughts of those who are wise according to worldly wisdom? (Verse 20b)

_____

19. (a) What comparison does the Lord use to convey the degree to which His thoughts and ways are higher than ours? (Isaiah 55:9a)

_____

(b) What question does God pose to people who are determined to spend their lives on earthly pursuits that are ultimately shallow and empty? (Verse 2a)

_____

_____

(c) What does God tell us to do in order to *eat what is good*? Complete the following:

Isaiah 55:2b: "_____ _____ _____ _____,

and eat what is good."

(d) When we incline our ears to God and come to Him, what will be the result for our souls? (Verse 3a)

_____

(e) What must a wicked, unrighteous person do in conjunction with returning to the Lord? (Verse 7a)

_____

_____

The main purpose of revelation is to lead us to
a supernatural experience in God's presence so that we can be transformed.

20. God has made known to us through the Scriptures many of His thoughts and ways.

    (a) How were the Scriptures given? (2 Timothy 3:16a)

    _____

    (b) What is the origin of scriptural prophecy? (2 Peter 1:21b)

    _____

    (c) By what route did scriptural prophecy *not* come about? (Verse 21a)

    _____

Part V: Revealed Knowledge

In addition to His written Word, God speaks to the heart of each believer through the Holy Spirit, and, as we have seen, He gives "now" words for today, or fresh revelation. Let us explore various avenues through which God has communicated fresh words of prophecy, starting with the revelation of Jesus Christ—the complete revelation and manifestation of the glory of the Father.

21. (a) After Peter declared that Jesus was the Messiah, what did Jesus tell him about how this knowledge had been revealed to him? (Matthew 16:17b)

_____

(b) What had *not* revealed this knowledge to Peter? (Verse 17a)

_____

22. What were some important means through which God bore witness to Jesus' deity and ministry, as well as to the revelation Jesus brought to the world from the Father? (Hebrews 2:4)

_____

_____

Miracles are outside the mental, sensorial,
or natural realm of knowledge, and science cannot explain them.

23. (a) In what way did Paul express that God is able to establish believers in their faith? Complete the following:

Romans 16:25–26a: "[God] *is able to establish you according to* _____

_____ _____ _____

_____ _____ _____, *according to the*

_____ _____ _____ _____

kept secret since the world began but now has been _____

_____...."

(b) The revelation that Gentiles, as well as Jews, could be fellow heirs with Christ and members of His body was not fully disclosed to God's people in the ages prior to Christ's coming. Through what avenue did Paul say this truth had been made known by God? Complete the following:

Ephesians 3:5b: "…*it has now been* _____ _____

_____ _____ *to His holy* _____ *and*

_____."

REFLECTIONS ON THE RELATIONSHIP BETWEEN SCRIPTURE AND REVELATION

The Scriptures do not change. They are the foundation of our belief and practice. However, apostles and prophets are still needed to establish churches, teach and strengthen believers, and give fresh revelation of the ways in which God is working in the present generation. We must realize that true revelation does not negate foundational biblical doctrine, or vice versa. A balance can be restored if we understand and incorporate both sound doctrine and fresh revelation in the church as we grow spiritually.

By nature, apostles have plans, designs, and projects from God that edify the church, advance the kingdom, and impact their surrounding communities. They have been given the spiritual map that will guide us, showing us the way to accomplish things.

Prophets express what God is saying and doing at the moment (see Amos 3:7); they also see and speak of the future and of the mysteries of God. Unless the prophetic ministry is operating in the church, people who long to connect with the supernatural may turn to counterfeit forms of spirituality, such as the occult. Today, many people lack direction, vision, and genuine prophetic revelation from God. This is the reason He is restoring to the church the ministries of the apostle and prophet. The ultimate goal is to see people walk in truth and not be destroyed.

When apostles and prophets are able to carry out their functions, the other three roles of the fivefold ministry (pastors, evangelists, and teachers) also function as they were meant to: the pastor takes care of the flock, the evangelist wins people for Jesus, and the teacher instructs the church—and all, as one, gather in the harvest of souls.

24. Besides the special roles of apostle and prophet (see Ephesians 4:11–12), there are four gifts that the Holy Spirit gives to certain believers, at His discretion, so that they may receive revelation from God to convey to His people. To discover these four gifts, complete the following:

    1 Corinthians 12:8, 10: "*...for to one is given* _____ _____

    _____ _____ *through the Spirit, to another* _____

    _____ _____ _____ *through the same*

    Spirit,...to another the working of miracles, to another _____,

    ...to another different kinds of tongues, to another _____

    _____ _____ _____."

<u>KEY DEFINITION</u>: Revelation is a fragment of divine knowledge that was not previously known by the person receiving it. For example, a "*word of knowledge*" (1 Corinthians 12:8) is a small portion of the total knowledge of God, given by the Holy Spirit in an instant.

---

25. (a) Paul told the Corinthians that they should "*pursue love, and desire spiritual gifts*" (1 Corinthians 14:1). What did he say they should especially desire? (Verse 1)

    _____

    (b) What does the person who prophesies "*speak...to men*"? (Verse 3)

    _____

    _____

Leaders without revelation or fresh knowledge from God
for their ministries will become irrelevant.

---

26. Besides the gift of prophecy mentioned in the below verse, what other means of receiving and communicating revelation does God bestow on His people through the Holy Spirit? Complete the following:

Joel 2:28: *"Your sons and your daughters shall prophesy, your old men shall*

_____ _____, *your young men shall* _____

_____."

27. What did Jesus say the Holy Spirit, or the *"Spirit of truth,"* would do for His followers? (John 16:13)

_____

_____

28. What statement by Jesus reinforces the difference between man's natural intellect and ability and God's thoughts and supernatural ability, which He conveys to us through revelation? (Luke 18:27)

_____

Revelation erases the borders of the impossible.

Conclusion

Revelation is spiritual knowledge about God and His ways that comes into our spirits for the purpose of moving us forward in His will and in our relationship with Him. It is a window from time into eternity and from eternity into time, bringing God's perspective to us human beings.

God's revelation always demands change on our part. We might not always understand the revelation we receive, but we do not have to understand it to obey it. All we have to do is receive it. Let us remember that, in earlier times, the prophets would announce messages from God that they did not always understand. And yet, they were obedient to declare them, and that which they declared came to pass—or will come to pass—in the Lord's time.

Ultimately, when we learn how to receive, walk in, and manifest God's revelation, we will not only have a deeper understanding of God and a more intimate relationship with Him, but we will also see healings, miracles, signs, wonders, and demonstrations of the power of God that bless His people and reveal His glory to the world.

Prayer of Activation

Father of glory, in the name of Jesus, we ask You to forgive us for having conformed to religion, legalism, and empty traditions. Release upon us a hunger and thirst for Your kingdom and glory. Use us as vessels of clay, chosen to manifest Your glory as we live our lives. Impart the fire of Your presence to us, right now, so we will never again be passive Christians but active and bold ones. We commit to make ourselves available to You, to surrender our bodies as living sacrifices, and to obey Your Word. We want to be a part of the remnant You are raising to manifest Your glory in these last days. We receive everything we have asked for, right now, as we go out into a lost world in the name and power of Jesus. Amen!

Action Steps

+ No matter what "impossible" situation you are facing, replace your natural thoughts with God's Word. Write down verses and passages that apply to your situation and review them daily, committing to memory as many as possible.

+ Similarly, ask the Holy Spirit to bring to your attention any negative, defeating thoughts as you go about your day. Then, as He reminds you, replace these thoughts with praise to God for His love, help, and strength.

EXPERIENCES WITH GOD'S GLORY

An Unborn Baby Brought Back to Life Through Revealed Knowledge

A woman who attends King Jesus Ministry testified that she had been three months pregnant when she received the devastating news that the baby she was carrying in her womb was dead. The baby's heartbeat could not be heard, even after several attempts by medical personnel to listen to it. This diagnosis was confirmed by several doctors who said the fetus had to be removed. Yet the woman decided not to accept the diagnosis of death; she appropriated the faith of God within her, believing for a miracle. Although she was afraid, the Holy Spirit filled her with faith. Because she was not willing to lose her child, she started attending the church's early-morning prayer meetings, led by Mrs. Ana Maldonado, who operates in the gift of prophecy.

One day, by a word of knowledge, Mrs. Maldonado perceived that she should pray for a woman who was having problems with her unborn child. When this woman came forward, she immediately felt movement in her womb. The child had returned to life by the powerful hand of God! The expectant mother cried tears of joy and gave thanks to Him. The word of knowledge given by the Holy Spirit saved the life of that child. The solution presented by the doctors had been abortion, but God's solution was resurrection and life.

The story does not end there. Near the end of this woman's pregnancy, she was told again by the doctor that the baby's heartbeat could not be heard and that the baby would certainly have to be removed this time. Both frustration and determination not to give up came upon the woman. Instead of surrendering, she said, "No! That is not true. I believe God, and I know He keeps my baby alive in my womb." New exams showed that the baby was fine and that the heartbeat was normal, but then she was told the baby would be born with Down syndrome due to the periods of time when the heartbeat had stopped. The baby's mother, full of the faith of God, again rejected the negative diagnosis. To the glory of God, her child is now a beautiful four-year-old boy who is healthy in mind and body. One word of knowledge, given by the Holy Spirit, resolved what the doctors were unable to do.

Study 6

From Foundational Doctrine to Revelation

"For in [the gospel of Christ] *the righteousness of God is revealed from faith to faith."*
—Romans 1:17

Introduction

How can we move from merely knowing doctrine about God to living in God's "now" revelation, through which His presence and glory manifest? After we have learned foundational Christian doctrine, we must believe and act on it. The Pharisees were a prominent Jewish group in the days of Jesus who were knowledgeable in theology and theory and kept their own practices very strictly. They interpreted the law of Moses but had a major problem: they did not often practice what they preached about that law. Consequently, they became "religious" people. They had an appearance of piety—frequently praying, fasting, and paying tithes—but they lacked moral authority. Jesus rebuked them and called their actions hypocritical. (See, for example, Matthew 23.) Since such behavior can easily spread to others, defiling them spiritually, Jesus told His disciples, *"Beware of the leaven* ["yeast" KJV, NIV] *of the Pharisees, which is hypocrisy"* (Luke 12:1).

If we take a close look at ourselves, as the church, we will find that things have not changed much since those days. Many people claim to believe in the supernatural; they say they want to see miracles, witness the power and the glory, and experience revival, but they hardly ever go beyond theory because they refuse to accept and live in the true power of God. This makes their conduct very similar to that of the Pharisees in not practicing what they preach. Therefore, in this study, we will explore how to move from foundational doctrine to "now" revelation and how to avoid the "yeast" of spiritual hypocrisy.

Study Questions

Part I: Build a Foundation of Basic Doctrine

1. (a) What is essential for us to know, which was known from childhood by Paul's son in the Lord, Timothy? Complete the following:

    2 Timothy 3:15a: "*...you have known* _____ _____

    _____....*"*

    (b) What are the Scriptures able to make us wise for? (Verse 15b)

    _____

2. (a) In what ways is Scripture profitable for us? (2 Timothy 3:16b)

    _____

    _____

    (b) What does it enable us to be thoroughly equipped for? (Verse 17)

    _____

3. What should new Christians, as well as those who have not yet matured in their faith, desire, and why should they desire it? (1 Peter 2:2)

    _____

Doctrine is the foundation we lay down to build a new believer;
this prepares him to receive revelation.

---

4. (a) Even though drinking the *"milk"* (Hebrews 5:12, 13) of God's Word is essential for coming to salvation and being established in our faith, what will happen if we continue to partake of only the milk of the Word and neglect to move on to *"solid food"* (verses 12, 14)? (Verse 13)

    _____

(b) To whom does *"solid food"* belong? (Hebrews 5:14)

_____

_____

5. After we have been established with a foundation of doctrine, what should we leave, and what should we go on to? (Hebrews 6:1a)

_____

Part II: Live What You Know

6. If we believe we can just hear the Word of God and not put it into practice, what are we doing? (James 1:22) Choose one of the following by circling the letter:

   (a) We are building up our faith.

   (b) We are deceiving ourselves.

   (c) We are deceiving God.

   (d) We are laying up treasures in heaven.

7. (a) To what did Jesus compare those who hear His teaching and put it into practice? (Matthew 7:24b)

   _____

   (b) What types of severe weather and their consequences did Jesus use as a metaphor for the storms of life that assail us? (Verse 25a)

   _____

   (c) Why did one house remain standing after all it had experienced? Complete the following:

   Verse 25b: *"...for it was _____ on the rock."*

Having intellectual knowledge of any biblical truth
does not imply that we have experienced it.

---

8. (a) In Jesus' explanation of the parable of the sower, He described people who receive God's Word with joy, although the inflexible, "rocky" state of their hearts makes it difficult for them to cultivate spiritual seed. For what reason do these people believe for a while but eventually fall away from the faith through temptation? (Luke 8:13b)

    _____

    (b) What occurs in the lives of people who are like *"thorns,"* who have heard God's Word but allow their faith to be *"choked with cares, riches, and pleasures of life"*? (Verse 14b)

    _____

    (c) What did Jesus emphasize about those whose lives are like *"good ground,"* who have *"heard the word with a noble and good heart"*? (Verse 15b)

    _____

9. List the various *"fruit of the Spirit"* we must continue to develop in our lives if we are to *"walk in the Spirit...and not fulfill the lust of the flesh"* (Galatians 5:16). (Verses 22–23a)

    _____

    _____

You cannot create a doctrine based on experience,
but all doctrine that comes from God will lead you to have an experience with Him.

---

10. (a) What are we to add to our faith? (2 Peter 1:5a)

    _____

    (b) What other attributes are we to add to our lives? (2 Peter 1:5b–7)

    _____

(c) If we *"abound"* in all these things, what will we avoid? (2 Peter 1:8b)

REFLECTIONS ON SPIRITUAL STAGNATION

People who are stuck in the basics of the Bible are not very open to receive revelation or revealed knowledge from God. Many of these people believe there is nothing else to know or experience. Others do not support the idea of learning more; they lack sufficient humility to receive anything new. Because they stay on the foundation of the faith instead of building on it, they remain spiritual "infants." These believers are usually the ones who criticize the movements and revivals of God and those who ignite them. Only when it is too late—after they have rejected, persecuted, and even betrayed those who have been anointed by God—do they sometimes realize that these were authentic movements.

There is a difference between (1) wanting to correct false/inaccurate theology or disorderliness due to unscriptural conduct and excesses, and (2) stifling a genuine move of God because of presuppositions and entrenched ways of thinking and acting. We must learn to discern between these different situations if we are to keep pace with what God is doing among His people today. If we don't, we may hinder not only our own spiritual health and growth but also those of others.

Part III: Go *"from Faith to Faith"*

As we mature in our faith, we are able to move more confidently from foundational doctrine to the "now" revelation of God, or His revelation for us today. Only when we are able to discern good from evil, and what is genuine from what is false, can we truly participate in the present moves of God. Revelation occurs in conjunction with manifestation, and it also leads to further manifestation. When God is revealed, some aspect of His nature or power will manifest.

11. How is the righteousness of God revealed? Complete the following:

Romans 1:17a: *"For in* [the gospel of Christ] *the righteousness of God is revealed*

_____ _____ ____ _____*."*

12. Faith always leads to some action—repentance, confession, worship, physical ministry to those who are suffering, healings, and so forth. What statement did James make to sum up the idea that belief in God's Word cannot remain theory but must be acted on? (James 2:26)

_____

It is easy to preach or teach something we do not have to demonstrate or prove.

13. When God entrusts His Word and His will to us, we become responsible for it as *"faithful and wise steward[s]"* (Luke 12:42). In relation to this, what must we keep in mind? Complete the following:

Luke 12:48b: *"For everyone to whom much is given, from him* _____

_____ _____ _____; *and to whom much has been*

committed, _____ _____ _____ _____ _____

_____ _____.*"*

14. The kingdom of God is demonstrated not by words but in what? (1 Corinthians 4:20)

_____

15. In what way did the Lord Jesus confirm the disciples' preaching after He ascended to heaven and sat down at the right hand of God? (Mark 16:20b)

_____

Miracles predispose the hearts of people to believe that God exists.

16. What did the apostles perform among the people as they ministered the gospel to them? (Acts 5:12a)

_____

17. What manifestations occurred when Philip preached Christ to the Samaritans? (Acts 8:7)

_____

_____

REFLECTIONS ON
SUPERNATURAL MANIFESTATIONS

When God is revealed, some invisible aspect of Him will manifest or make itself known to the human senses, causing great impact and transformation. Manifestations are *signs*; they are not doctrines. When evaluating a manifestation, we need to determine if God is taking the initiative and doing the work. We will know this is the case if the work is consistent with His nature and character and if it produces the same in the people involved. We need to ask questions such as these: "Does the manifestation go against the Scriptures?" "Did the experience promote a love for God in the person who experienced it?" "Do I have peace about this situation?" "Do I sense the confirmation of the Holy Spirit?" God wants to lead us into newer, deeper, and more extensive territories in Him, and only if we have a solid base from which to expand can we ensure the continued stability of our faith.

18. What reason did Paul give the Corinthians for why his speech and preaching to them *"were not done with persuasive words of human wisdom, but in demonstration of the Spirit and of power"* (1 Corinthians 2:4)? (Verse 5)

_____

19. In the previous study, we focused on four of the nine gifts of the Spirit that are specifically related to revelation—the word of wisdom, the word of knowledge, prophecy, and the interpretation of tongues. What are the remaining five gifts, which God gives to the church to enable its members to receive and minister various aspects of His power? (1 Corinthians 12:9–10)

_____

_____

Where genuine revelation from God exists, there must be visible manifestations that confirm its divine origin.

Part IV: Seek Fresh Revelation

We require God's wisdom and knowledge for contemporary problems and needs whose solutions may not be spelled out exactly in Scripture. This takes fresh revelation from God, which must be sought in faithfulness, with pure motivations, and according to biblical guidelines. For these cases, especially, we can see the necessity of first establishing a foundation of sound doctrine through which our spiritual senses may be *"exercised to discern both good and evil"* (Hebrews 5:14). In the next few questions, we will examine how the early Christians handled some of their contemporary problems and needs, including solving disputes and controversies according to God's will and seeking where God wanted them to minister at a particular time.

20. (a) Agabus was a Christian from Jerusalem who had the ministry gift of prophecy. What forthcoming crisis did the Holy Spirit reveal to him when he went to Antioch, so that the believers could be aware of it ahead of time? (Acts 11:28)

_____

(b) What did the disciples do in response to this news? (Verses 29–30)

_____

_____

21. (a) What did the Holy Spirit subsequently instruct the prophets and teachers of the church at Antioch to do? (Acts 13:2b)

_____

_____

(b) What had the prophets and teachers been doing when they received this revelation of direction? (Verse 2a)

_____

REFLECTIONS ON PROPHECY

To prophesy is to speak from the perspective of God, and the source of that perspective is the Holy Spirit, who reveals what is in the mind or heart of the Father. (See 1 Corinthians 2:10.) True prophecy will always provide *"edification and exhortation and comfort"* (1 Corinthians 14:3) in order to lead people to see what God sees and to walk in a reality that is superior to the natural. It is like taking a leap into the future in God or declaring that glorious future in the present.

22. (a) The apostles and elders in Jerusalem wrote to the Gentile converts to delineate what aspects of the Jewish law these Gentiles would be required to follow as believers in Jesus. What phrase did they use to explain how they had arrived at their answer to this controversial issue? (Acts 15:28a)

_____

(b) What did Paul say had prompted him to go to the church in Jerusalem to discuss this issue concerning the Gentile believers with the apostles and elders? Complete the following:

Galatians 2:2a: *"And I went up* _____ _____*."*

(c) With whom in the church did Paul consult privately, to affirm the validity of the gospel message that he had been preaching among the Gentiles? (Galatians 2:2b)

_____

23. (a) Why didn't Paul, Silas, and Timothy go to Asia to preach the Word? (Acts 16:6)

_____

(b) Why didn't they go into Bithynia? (Verse 7)

_____

(c) Following these prohibitions, Paul received a vision in the night. How did Luke, the author of the book of Acts, describe this vision? (Acts 16:9b)

_____

_____

(d) After Paul received the vision, what did Paul, Silas, and Timothy conclude, and what did they do? (Verse 10)

_____

_____

Part V: Discern False Teachings and Manifestations

24. (a) When a prophecy is given among a body of believers, what biblical instructions do we have for determining whether that prophecy is from God? (1 Corinthians 14:29; 1 John 4:1)

_____

_____

_____

(b) What are the spirits of the prophets subject to? (1 Corinthians 14:32)

_____

(c) What aspect of the nature of God does this approach correspond to? Complete the following:

Verse 33a: _"For God is not the author of confusion but of _____...."_

(d) What statement sums up the way we are to conduct ourselves in the use of spiritual gifts? (1 Corinthians 14:40)

_____

25. (a) After we have "tested all things" in regard to prophecies and other revelation, what are we to do? (1 Thessalonians 5:21b)

_____

(b) What caution have we been given, reminding us not to hinder the Lord's work by undue apprehension over spiritual gifts or excessive "testing"? (Verse 19)

_____

(c) What are we to earnestly desire? (1 Corinthians 14:39a)

_____

(d) What are we not to forbid? (Verse 39b)

_____

26. (a) What supernatural manifestation did the devil tempt Jesus to effect to "prove" His identity as God's Son? (Matthew 4:3)

_____

(b) How did Jesus respond to the devil in resisting this temptation? (Verse 4)

_____

_____

Every time we use our gifts or anointing to exalt our egos, to prove how "spiritual" we are, to seek gain, or to obtain a position, we are commercializing the anointing.

27. What word recurs in the following Scriptures, indicating one of Jesus' primary motivations for helping people and performing healing and miracles on their behalf? (Matthew 9:36; 14:14; 15:32; 20:34)

_____

28. Paul talked about those who preached Christ from *"envy and strife,"* as well as others who did so out of *"good will"* (Philippians 1:15). What incentive did each of these groups have? Complete the following:

Philippians 1:16–17a: *"The former preach Christ from* _____

_____*...but the latter out of* _____*...."*

29. (a) What did Simon, the former sorcerer, offer to Peter and John because he wanted to have the power of bestowing the Holy Spirit on people? (Acts 8:18b)

_____

(b) What did Peter discern were the underlying reasons for Simon's erroneous request, which caused Simon to think the gift of the Holy Spirit could be obtained in this way? (Verse 23)

_____

30. (a) What is a prerequisite for having the ability to recognize whether a teaching or doctrine comes from God or from man—the same prerequisite Jesus gave the religious leaders who inquired about His doctrine? Complete the following:

John 7:17a: *"If anyone* _____ _____ _____ _____ [God's]

_____*...."*

(b) What does someone who speaks from himself seek? (Verse 18a)

_____

(c) What did Jesus say that He sought? (Verse 18b)

_____

Revelation introduces us to the manifestation of the glory of God;
without it, the glory cannot be seen.

Conclusion

The purpose of doctrine is to establish believers solidly in the faith. Once the foundation of doctrine is laid, we build on it. Every such transition implies risk because it involves moving from a known location to an unknown one. Most people fear the unknown; therefore, they prefer to stay in one place where it is comfortable and convenient. However, people who do not move—those without revelation—may never experience the power of God flowing through them. We must desire to go to higher levels, other dimensions; to expand into new territories; to move to greater realms of faith, anointing, glory, growth, and maturity. Christian living is designed to be a daily adventure because we must meet every new challenge with faith. If we conform—settling for where we are now—we become stagnant, and this does not please God.

God's glory is with us on the earth, just as the Scripture says. (See Habakkuk 2:14.) The only thing we need to access and manifest the glory is the knowledge of God as revealed by the Holy Spirit. Men and women who have moved in God's supernatural power and have been used by Him to do miracles, signs, and wonders have had a revelation given by His Spirit; this is what made them different from others.

You don't have to be a preacher or a leader in your church to begin to receive revelation and to act on it. As He did with the early church, the Lord is doing in the twenty-first century: He is using common people to carry out His will on the earth. Will you allow God to work through you?

Prayer of Activation

Father of glory, thank You for the gifts of the Spirit and the ministry gifts You have imparted to the church. We ask You to activate them in us as we "fan them into flame" in anticipation of the work of the Holy Spirit in our lives. We make ourselves available to receive Your revelation and power for this generation. In Jesus' name, amen.

Action Steps

- Perhaps you have not often made time for regular Bible reading, study, and meditation, so that you lack a strong biblical foundation. If this is the case, then build your house on the "rock" by making the study of the Word of God a priority in your life, even after you have completed this Bible study.

♦ Since spiritual maturity and integrity come from acting on what we have already learned from God's Word, make a commitment today to obey the full will of God. Start today by being obedient to God in an area where you have been avoiding His promptings either to do something or to stop doing something. Ask Him for grace and power by His Spirit to obey Him fully. As you obey in this area, choose another area and do the same.

♦ When you seek God in prayer, ask Him to reveal an aspect of His nature or power to you through His Word, through a gift of the Spirit, or though another supernatural manifestation. Then, be continually open to receive His revelation knowledge.

EXPERIENCES WITH GOD'S GLORY

A Ministry of Miracles in the Supernatural Power of God

In 2005, Pastors José Luis and Rosa Margarita López of New International Generation Church in Mexico had two hundred members after twelve years of ministry. They were preparing to quit. Years previously, God had rescued José Luis from alcoholism, drug addiction, and psychotropic medications (medicines that treat the mind), and Margarita had been delivered from bitterness and unforgiveness toward her family. They began to serve Jesus passionately, and, years later, they were anointed and sent out by their church as pastors to establish their own independent church. José quit his profession as an architect, and Margarita quit her law practice. They also closed their construction business and sold all the equipment in preparation to serve the Lord. Undoubtedly, God had called them. However, they were dealing with a ministry that did not bear much fruit, regardless of how hard they tried. They did not know what else to do. They wanted to serve God and see greater results, but there they were, stuck, unable to move forward! They had also lost their home, and their relationship with their son was not going well. They had reached a point in their ministry where they said, "Lord, this is it. We give up!"

After being trained and equipped in the supernatural power and glory of God, they began to change. They put themselves under spiritual accountability and surrendered to God to be delivered from everything that had been hindering them, to be edified, and to receive the impartation of His supernatural power. God restored their family and then their congregation. By the end of the year, their ministry had grown to fifteen hundred people, and it soon reached twenty-five hundred active members.

Today, they have a solid congregation of over nine thousand members. Their son, Rodrigo, also accepted the call of God on his life and is now the youth pastor. They are impacting their nation. One reason for their impact is that Pastor José Luis began to practice "supernatural evangelism." He no longer relies on man-made methods of evangelizing but allows the Spirit of God to work through him to draw people to the Lord.

Also, since the day Rodrigo accepted the call of God, the youth group has grown exponentially. After being trained and equipped to walk in the supernatural power and glory of God, he has trained and equipped thousands of Mexican young people in the same way, and the Lord has responded through miracles and wonders. One weekend, Pastor Rodrigo led the youth of the church to visit the hospitals in the city, where they prayed for the sick. Patients who had cancer were healed. Those who had undergone open-heart surgery were also fully healed. People who were waiting in the emergency room were healed. The doctors could not find anything wrong with them. God healed everyone! As a result, the next Sunday, those who had received healing came to the church and testified. This is what the glory of God is doing in the world today.

THREE DIMENSIONS OF THE SUPERNATURAL

"We do not look at the things which are seen, but at the things which are not seen."
—2 Corinthians 4:18

Introduction

God is everywhere—He is omnipresent—but, as we have learned, He does not manifest His glory everywhere. His glory manifests in visible and tangible form only where people worship Him in spirit and in truth (see John 4:23) and where they receive His revelation by faith. Receiving revelation requires understanding the interrelationship between three dimensions of the supernatural: (1) faith, (2) anointing, and (3) glory. In this study, we will look at each of these areas, and then, in the next study, we will discover essential steps to transition from the anointing to the glory.

Study Questions

Part I: Faith

1. What has God dealt to each believer? (Romans 12:3b)

   _____

2. How does the Bible define faith? (Hebrews 11:1)

   _____

<u>KEY DEFINITION:</u> The word *"faith"* in Hebrews 11:1 comes from the Greek word *pistis*, meaning "conviction" or "firm persuasion."

---

3. While we live on the earth, how are we to *"walk"* in such a way that we may remain connected to God in the spiritual realm? Complete the following:

   2 Corinthians 5:7: *"For* _____ _____ _____ _____*, not by sight."*

4. (a) As we live according to faith, what do we not "look" at, and what do we "look" at? (2 Corinthians 4:18a)

   _____

   (b) For what reason should we take this perspective? (Verse 18b)

   _____

Faith was given to us so we could reach beyond time into eternity.

---

5. Why is faith so essential to our relationship with God? (Hebrews 11:6a)

   _____

6. (a) When we ask for things in prayer, what are we to believe? (Mark 11:24)

   _____

   (b) When we believe this, what will be the outcome? (Verse 24b)

   _____

7. What did Jesus exhort His disciples to have? (Mark 11:22)

   _____

REFLECTIONS ON THE MEANING OF FAITH

Faith has nothing to do with presumption or optimism. It is the confidence that the Lord will act because He cannot lie or fail to keep His Word. (See, for example, 1 Samuel 15:29; Isaiah 55:10–11.) If He said it, we can rest assured that it will be as He has said. Faith is a prerequisite for seeing the glory because having faith means we believe in what God can do. It is the ability to believe the "unreasonable" or "impossible."

A more literal translation of Jesus' statement *"Have faith in God"* (Mark 11:22) is "Have God's faith." Jesus did not ask us to have faith *in* God; He was saying that God gives us a measure of faith that belongs to Him. Because our human nature is incapable of generating faith on its own, we must take hold of God's faith.

8. Since Christ lives in us, in what manner are we to live our lives, just as the apostle Paul did? (Galatians 2:20b)

9. In the previous study, we saw that we are to progress *"from faith to faith,"* as Paul wrote in Romans 1:17. What statement did Paul quote from the book of Habakkuk when writing that verse? (Habakkuk 2:4b)

Part II: Anointing

We need to walk by faith in every circumstance and realm of our lives, including our spiritual anointing from God. The anointing is the power of God working through us to do what He wants done on earth. Anointings are also given to set apart certain men and women for ministry roles and to enable them to carry out their callings.

10. In the Old Testament, people whom God had chosen and set apart for special roles were often anointed with oil. What happened to David when the prophet Samuel anointed him with oil to be the next king of Israel? (1 Samuel 16:13)

11. When Bezalel was called by God to a special task, what endowment of the Spirit of God did he receive, enabling him to create intricate, beautiful ornamentation for the tabernacle and the ark of the testimony? (Exodus 31:3–5)

    _____

    _____

    _____

12. In the Old Testament, the Holy Spirit would temporarily come *upon* specific people so they could fulfill various purposes of God. After Jesus' death, resurrection, and ascension, all believers were given the privilege of having the Holy Spirit live *within* them. How did John describe the Spirit's presence in our lives? (1 John 2:20a)

    _____

13. (a) Shortly before He ascended to heaven, Jesus *"breathed"* on His disciples and said, *"Receive the Holy Spirit"* (John 20:22). Yet what did He say His disciples would also soon experience in relation to the Holy Spirit? (Acts 1:5b)

    _____

    (b) What would they receive as a result? (Verse 8a)

    _____

    (c) What occurred when they had this experience on the day of Pentecost? (Acts 2:4)

    _____

    _____

14. (a) Peter and John learned that the Samaritan believers had been baptized only in the name of Jesus but that the Holy Spirit had not yet *"fallen upon…them"* (Acts 8:16). What did Peter and John do next, and what followed their action? (Verse 17)

_____

_____

(b) While Peter was preaching the gospel to Cornelius and other Gentiles, what happened to all who heard him? (Acts 10:44)

_____

(c) What was the evidence that this event had occurred? (Verse 46)

_____

(d) When Paul was in Ephesus, he met some followers of John the Baptist who had never heard of the Holy Spirit. After these followers heard the complete gospel, believed in Jesus, and were baptized in water, what did Paul do? (Acts 19:6a)

_____

(e) What happened next? (Verse 6b)

_____

15. The Holy Spirit has given all believers a measure of anointing to enable them to fulfill God's will for their lives. What did Paul explain about this anointing? Complete the following:

(a) 1 Corinthians 12:7: *"But the* _____ _____

_____ _____ _____ _____ *to each one* _____

_____ _____ ____ _____.*"*

(b) Verse 11: *"But one and the same Spirit works all these things,*

_____ _____ _____ _____

_____ _____ _____ _____.*"*

16. (a) As a review, list the five roles included in the "ministry gifts" that Jesus has given. (Ephesians 4:11)

    _____

    (b) For what purposes does He give these ministry gifts? (Verse 12)

    _____

    _____

17. What did the leaders of the church in Antioch do in commissioning Paul and Barnabas for the special work to which God had called them? (Acts 13:3)

    _____

    _____

The anointing is God's power working through us to do what He wants done on earth.

---

18. (a) When Jesus sent out the twelve apostles to minister the gospel in various towns, what practice did they follow that "set apart to God," as it were, those who were sick to receive God's healing power and also served as a symbol of the Spirit's work in their lives? (Mark 6:13b)

    _____

    (b) What instructions did the apostle James write to the early Christians in regard to a believer who is sick? (James 5:14)

    _____

    _____

    (c) What will save the sick person, so that the Lord raises him up? (Verse 15a)

    _____

(d) If a sick person has committed sins, what will also occur? (James 5:15b)

_____

19. (a) What did Jesus perceive when the woman with the flow of blood touched the hem of His robe? Complete the following:

Luke 8:46: "*Somebody touched Me, for I perceived* _____ _____

_____ _____ _____."

(b) According to Jesus, what made the woman well? (Verse 48b)

_____

A minister of God cannot force the anointing on people—
they have to appropriate it by faith.

REFLECTIONS ON FAITH AND THE ANOINTING

It has been my experience that each measure of anointing given to a believer is made up of various levels. One level is equivalent to a "step" that must be taken or ascended as we progress in our ability to move in that anointing and to grow spiritually in relation to it. No step can be skipped, because each step represents an essential aspect of maturity in spiritual matters. We must go from step to step, or from level to level, without missing one, until we reach the level at which we have fully developed the measure of the anointing we have received. When we reach the last level, we can do nothing further in terms of our anointing—we have reached the fullness of that measure. At this point, the only option available to us is to enter into the glory. Having the anointing is not the same thing as moving in the glory, which includes all of God's attributes. The anointing is a *part* of God, operating through us.

Another aspect of anointing is that the faith of one believer can draw out the anointing of another believer. In other words, a person can exercise faith that puts a spiritual "demand" on the anointing of another person to operate in that anointing. For example, a preacher may need to stop in the middle of his message and pray for someone in the congregation who is exercising faith, thinking, *I believe that he will come now and lay hands on me for healing because I need a miracle.* Faith attracts the anointing; in this way, faith and the anointing work together.

20. Describe the anointing Jesus had on His life. (Luke 4:18–19)

_____

_____

_____

21. (a) What did Peter say that God had anointed Jesus with? (Acts 10:38a)

_____

(b) What did Jesus do in accordance with this anointing? (Verse 38b)

_____

22. Recall what Jesus said about those who believe in Him. (John 14:12b)

_____

_____

Part III: Glory

In the third dimension of the supernatural, God acts in His sovereignty, without the participation of human beings directly exercising their faith or anointing. However, our faith is often a prerequisite to seeing God Himself in the dimension of His glory. Faith and the anointing prepare us to receive the glory, which is God's manifest presence. Let us look at some examples of the activity of God in His sovereignty.

23. (a) In a list of the descendants of Adam that records the age at which people died, what unusual and sovereign act of the Lord is mentioned in relation to Enoch, indicating that he did not experience physical death? Complete the following:

Genesis 5:24b: "...*and* [Enoch] *was not,* _____ _____ _____

_____."

(b) How does the Bible describe Enoch's relationship with the Lord? (Genesis 5:24a)

_____

The glory is the manifest presence—the shekinah—of God.

---

24. As a review, what manifestation of the presence of the Lord occurred after Moses completed the new tabernacle? (Exodus 40:34)

_____

25. (a) What happened after the prophet Elijah prayed to the Lord and asked Him to show that He was the almighty and true God and that Baal was a counterfeit god? (1 Kings 18:38)

_____

_____

(b) How did the Israelites, who were observing this manifestation, respond to it? (Verse 39)

_____

People know they are moving in a dimension of the glory of God
when they no longer need to use their faith or anointing.

REFLECTIONS ON
THE ANOINTING AND THE GLORY

While God has anointed us to fulfill His purposes, He also acts independently of us at times, Thus, we need to learn how these two situations are distinct and how they work together. Some people say, "I never minister unless God tells me to do so," believing they are imitating Jesus, who said, _"The Son can do nothing of Himself, but what He sees the Father do; for whatever He does, the Son also does in like manner"_ (John 5:19). What happens is that these people keep waiting for God to show up in His glory to speak to them, and they end up doing nothing. What they don't realize is that hearing from God in that manner is only one dimension, or aspect, of the way He works. For example, there are certain things that we have already been instructed to do, such as to spread the good news of the gospel to those who have not heard it. Luke 9:2 says, "[Jesus] *sent* [His disciples] *to preach the kingdom of God and to heal the sick.*"

We don't say, "Well, I'll go evangelize when God tells me to." That's taking things to an extreme. Of course, we must be listening for His guidance as we tell others about Jesus. And we should wait on God to see if He chooses to manifest His glory. But if He doesn't, then we are to operate according to the anointing He has already given us.

---

26. (a) What analogies does the book of Judges use to depict the number of Midianites, Amalekites, and *"people of the East,"* along with their camels, who had come against Israel in the time of Gideon? (Judges 7:12b)

_____

_____

(b) How many Israelite men were chosen by the Lord to stand against these enemies? (Verse 7a)

_____

(c) What "weapons" did the soldiers use? (Verse 16b)

_____

(d) How did they use these "weapons"? (Verse 20a)

_____

_____

(e) What did the soldiers cry out? (Verse 20b)

_____

(f) What happened to the combined enemy army? (Judges 7:21b)

_____

27. (a) What did the angel tell Mary concerning the way in which God would cause her to become the mother of the Messiah? (Luke 1:35a)

_____

_____

(b) What did Mary say as she accepted God's sovereign purpose? (Verse 38a)

_____

_____

We work under the anointing but rest in God's glory.

---

28. (a) When discussing her brother's death with Jesus, how long did Martha say that Lazarus had been dead? (John 11:39b)

_____

(b) What was Jesus' reply to Martha after hearing this? (Verse 40)

_____

(c) After Jesus prayed, what happened, demonstrating the glory of God? (Verse 44a)

_____

(d) What did Jesus say should be done for Lazarus? (Verse 44b)

_____

29. (a) God's sovereign outpouring of His glory on the day of Pentecost produced massive conversions to Christ. How many people were added to the kingdom of God in that one day after hearing the disciples glorify God in *"tongues"* and listening to Peter's proclamation of the gospel? (Acts 2:41b)

_____

(b) Not long afterward, Peter and John healed a lame man at the temple in the name of Jesus, and Peter preached the gospel to the crowds who gathered in amazement. Following these events, what was the total number of men who believed in Jesus? (Acts 4:4)

_____

The only movement able to generate transformation in society is the outpouring of the glory of God.

---

30. What does it mean to experience God's glory? Complete the following:

Hebrews 6:4b–5: *"…[We] have become partakers of the Holy Spirit, and have tasted the good word of God and the* _____ _____ _____

_____ _____ _____*."*

Conclusion

We must progress from faith to the anointing to the glory. As we learned in a previous study, God manifests His presence and glory according to His sovereignty. He does what He wants, when He wants, and in the way He wants, without depending on our faith, gifts, or anointing. I strongly believe that the last move of God upon the earth will not come through a man or woman but directly from God. We will experience the *"powers of the age to come"* (Hebrews 6:5) as He brings to completion His plan of redemption and the culmination of all things to make way for the new heavens and earth. Let us continue to seek Him with all our hearts so that we may find Him and experience the fullness of His glory.

Prayer of Activation

Father of glory, we walk by faith and not by sight. May we exercise the faith You have given us, so that we may believe and see Your glory. Anoint us anew to minister to others according to Your gifts and power. And let us experience Your glory as You act sovereignly in marvelous ways in our midst! In Jesus' name, amen.

Action Steps

+ As you pray for the concerns in your life according to God's Word, actively believe that you receive the answers to your prayers, just as Jesus instructed us in Mark 11:24.

+ Pray for someone you know who is sick. Ask that person if you or the leadership of his church may anoint him with oil in the name of the Lord, explaining the biblical instruction to do so from James 5:14–15.

EXPERIENCES WITH GOD'S GLORY

Woman Delivered from a Spirit of Suicide
After a Self-Inflicted Gunshot Wound to the Head

Franklin learned that one of his coworkers, who had been struggling with deep depression, had put a gun to her head and shot herself. She survived and underwent surgery to have the bullet extracted. Franklin felt led by the Lord to visit her at the hospital and pray for her, but he did not think he would be allowed to enter the intensive care unit where she was. When he arrived, he saw people crying; everyone feared the worst. A nurse intercepted him and asked, "Who are you and what are you doing here?" He answered, "God sent me. I have come to pray for her, and then I will leave." The nurse said, "Go ahead and pray. And, if possible, anoint her with oil."

The young lady had been in a coma for a week without reacting to any stimuli, but, after Franklin released words of life over her, she began to recuperate rapidly. Suddenly, she started to move her hands and feet; she even tried to remove the tubes that connected her to the monitors and other machines. Everyone was amazed! The next day, this woman was disconnected from the machines and released from the hospital. She accepted the Lord and was delivered from depression and the spirit of suicide. God rescued this young woman from the grip of death! He will use anyone who makes himself available to Him. Where the revelation of the will of God abounds, His glory will manifest!

Study 8

TRANSITIONING FROM THE ANOINTING TO THE GLORY

"That the God of our Lord Jesus Christ, the Father of glory, may give to you the spirit of wisdom and revelation in the knowledge of Him."
—Ephesians 1:17

Introduction

Revelation, or revealed knowledge, leads us to experience God's glory. And we receive revelation as we draw closer to Him. Most of us stay in the realm of faith and the anointing. Yet, to transition from the anointing to glory, we must recognize who receives revelation, develop a redeemed mind-set according to God's perspective, allow God to be God, respect the glory, and realize that revelation comes only to those who truly hunger and thirst for Him.

Study Questions

Part I: Who Receives Revelation?

1. (a) To whom does God disclose His *"secret"*? Complete the following:

    Psalm 25:14: *"The secret of the* LORD *is with* _____ _____ _____

    [reverence] _____, *and He will* _____ _____ _____

    _____."

(b) What did Moses tell the Israelites concerning those to whom God's revelation belongs, as well as the reason why He gives it to them? Complete the following:

Deuteronomy 29:29: *"The secret things belong to the LORD our God, but those things which are revealed belong to* _____ _____ _____ _____

_____ _____, *that we may*

_____ _____ _____ _____ _____ _____

_____.*"*

2. Through what means does God reveal what He has prepared for those who love Him? (1 Corinthians 2:10a)

_____

For lack of revelation and knowledge,
many believers have never experienced the glory of God.

---

3. What did God tell Jeremiah He would do if he called on Him? (Jeremiah 33:3)

_____

_____

4. What do we need to pray daily that the *"Father of glory"* will give us, as Paul prayed for the Ephesians? (Ephesians 1:17b)

_____

REFLECTIONS ON COMMUNION WITH GOD

God shares His secrets only with those who reverence and respect Him—not with His enemies, who despise and reject His secrets, and not with those who are complacent toward Him and His ways. Intimate communion with God is part of the covenant we have with Him through Jesus Christ, and He gives His revelation to those who are humble in heart. When people do not reverence the Lord, they are not able to receive truths taught from the Word of God by preachers and teachers. In such cases, their failure to receive God's truths is not due to a lack on the part of the preachers or teachers but to the state of these people's hearts.

Part II: Jesus Opened the Way to Ongoing Revelation

5. Under the old covenant, only the high priest could enter the Most Holy Place, or Holy of Holies, in the temple once a year, on the Day of Atonement, to make restitution for the people's sins. The Holiest was separated from the rest of the temple by a curtain, or veil, because that is where God's presence was manifested above the mercy seat of the ark of the covenant. What happened to this veil in the temple at the very moment when Jesus died on the cross? (Matthew 27:51a)

   _____

6. (a) How has Jesus enabled us to be reconciled to God? Complete the following:

   Hebrews 6:20: "*…the forerunner has entered for us, even Jesus,* _____

   _____ _____ _____ _____

   according to the order of Melchizedek."

   (b) With what did Jesus enter the Most Holy Place, or heaven, "*having obtained eternal redemption*" (Hebrews 9:12)? (Verse 12a)

   _____

   (c) How often did He enter, and for whom? Complete the following:

   Verse 12b: "*He entered the Most Holy Place* _____ _____

   _____.…*"*

7. Through our faith and hope in Jesus, what can we now also enter? Complete the following:

   Hebrews 6:19b: "*…*_____ _____ *behind the veil.*"

8. (a) Because of what Jesus has done for us, in what manner may we enter the Holiest, and by what means? (Hebrews 10:19a)

_____

(b) When we are in God's presence, in what way are we to draw near to Him? (Verse 22a)

_____

9. Now that we have peace with God and access into His grace through our faith in Jesus Christ, what do we rejoice in? (Romans 5:2)

_____

KEY DEFINITION: In Hebrews 10:19, the word translated *"boldness"* is the Greek word *parrhesia*, which means "freedom of speech; unreserved in speech; to speak openly and with honesty." This definition helps us to understand that merely "believing" in what Jesus did for us is not enough. We must say it, declare it, decree it. The redeemed must testify saying, "I am redeemed." (See Psalm 107:2.)

Part III: Develop a New Mind-set

10. Our redemption in Jesus, by which we can enter the presence of God, involves a new way of thinking. What did God say about the covenant He would make with His people through Christ? (Hebrews 10:16b)

_____

_____

11. With what three aspects of our being did Jesus say we are to love God completely? (Matthew 22:37)

_____

12. Since we were *"raised with Christ"* (Colossians 3:1), on what should we *"set"* our minds? (Colossians 3:2)

_____

13. Using Jesus' model prayer as a pattern, what should we should pray as a reflection of our new mind-set in Christ? (Matthew 6:10)

_____

14. According to Jesus, what are possible to those who believe in God? (Mark 9:23b)

_____

When the spirit of wisdom and revelation is absent, the church imparts only information and natural knowledge, and people are not transformed.

Part IV: Allow God to Be God

15. (a) What are we to do in recognition of God? (Psalm 46:10a)

_____

(b) Where will God be exalted? (Verse 10b)

_____

16. (a) Whose example was Jesus following as He performed specific healings and miracles? (John 5:19b)

_____

(b) Why did the Father show the Son everything that He did? (Verse 20a)

_____

17. (a) What did Jesus say in the garden of Gethsemane that reflected His inner commitment to surrender His life fully to God and His sovereign purposes? (Matthew 26:39b)

_____

(b) What must we do, in order to follow in His footsteps? (Matthew 16:24b)

_____

(c) What will happen to those who desire to save their lives, and what will happen to those who lose their lives for Christ's sake? (Verse 25)

_____

18. By what did Jesus learn obedience, even though He was the Son of God? (Hebrews 5:8b)

_____

No knowledge or revelation becomes ours until it is obeyed and practiced.

---

19. What mind-set did Christ have, which we are also to have? (See Philippians 2:5.) Complete the following:

(a) Philippians 2:7: "*...but* _____ _____ _____ _____

_____ , *taking the form of a bondservant....*"

(b) What did Christ do, which we are to emulate? Complete the following:

Verse 8: "*And being found in appearance as a man, He* _____

_____ *and* _____

_____ _____ _____ _____

_____ . *...*"

Part V: Respect the Glory

20. (a) What did Uzzah the priest do when the cart that was carrying the ark of the covenant to Jerusalem swayed? (2 Samuel 6:6)

_____

_____

(b) What did God do to Uzzah as a result of his action, and why? (Verse 7)

_____

_____

REFLECTIONS ON UZZAH'S PUNISHMENT

The ark of the covenant that was carried to Jerusalem on a cart pulled by oxen was not transported according to God's instructions to Moses. It should have been carried by the Levites (see Deuteronomy 10:8), raised upon their shoulders by wooden poles (see Exodus 25:13–15). In the Old Testament, not even the priests were allowed to touch the ark or to examine its contents. Although Uzzah belonged to the tribe of Levi, he failed to respect the presence of God, which the ark represented, when he took hold of it. This incident should demonstrate for us that we are not to become casual about the presence of God in our lives or in our midst when we gather together as believers; that is an atrocity! Uzzah's fate teaches us to be reverent toward God. He is the only One worthy of worship and honor. These verses ultimately reveal the importance of knowing and understanding the glory of God so that we can walk in it, live in it, and experience it without offending Him. Otherwise, we expose ourselves to discipline and punishment, perhaps even death.

21. (a) What statement did King Nebuchadnezzar make about the kingdom of Babylon, and about himself? (Daniel 4:30)

_____

_____

(b) What punishment did God tell the king he would undergo for taking the glory for himself? (Verses 31–32a)

_____

_____

(c) This punishment would last for seven years, until the king knew a certain truth. What is that truth? (Daniel 4:32b)

_____

_____

(d) What is God able to do to those who walk in pride? (Verse 37b)

_____

(e) Whom did Nebuchadnezzar bless, praise, and honor after the seven years? Why? (Verse 34b)

_____

_____

22. (a) Centuries later, when King Herod Agrippa I of Palestine sat on his throne dressed in royal apparel, what did the people shout? (Acts 12:22)

_____

(b) What happened to Herod, and why? (Verse 23a)

_____

_____

23. What two offenses did Ananias and Sapphira commit against the Holy Spirit, resulting in their deaths? (Acts 5:3a, 9a)

_____

24. (a) During Jesus' transfiguration, Peter told Jesus that he would make three tabernacles—one for Jesus, one for Moses, and one for Elijah. Did he realize what he was saying? (Luke 9:33b)

_____

(b) What did the *"voice"* from the cloud say to Peter and the other disciples to emphasize the respect, glory, and honor Jesus alone was due? (Luke 9:35b)

_____

Part VI: Revelation Comes to Those Who Hunger and Thirst

25. What does Jesus promise to the person who loves Him and keeps His Word? (John 14:23b)

_____

26. Whom did Jesus say would be spiritually filled? (Matthew 5:6a)

_____

27. (a) What did Jesus say had been given to His disciples? (Matthew 13:11a)

_____

(b) Why do certain people lack this ability? (Verse 15a)

_____

(c) Why did Jesus say the disciples' eyes and ears were blessed? (Verse 16)

_____

<u>KEY DEFINITION</u>: Spiritually speaking, a *mystery* is something that cannot be perceived or known through natural means. It is knowledge that God alone has, and the only way human beings may have access to it is by revelation of the Holy Spirit.

Knowledge of the glory belongs to the realm of the mysteries of God.

Conclusion

Jesus showed us the way of obedience as the only path to reach maturity and enjoy eternal life; no rebellious person will enter the kingdom of heaven. Jesus had to set aside His own will to do the will of the Father. When He denied Himself and went to the cross to fulfill the Father's purpose for salvation, it was the zenith of all the self-denial He had exercised throughout His life on earth.

We, too, must deny ourselves in order to fulfill the Father's will for us. We must say no to our rebellious, sinful nature. When the ego says, "I want," we must respond, "No!" We cannot negotiate with the ego. It must be put to death. It must die so that Jesus can live through us!

All of God's children must also follow Jesus' example to be perfected in holiness through suffering. (See Hebrews 5:8–9.) In the church today, the concept of suffering is rarely mentioned; in many cases, it is even rejected. Some people have reached the extreme of labeling it as a bad word because they refuse to accept the suffering that accompanies full obedience to God and His Word. Yet when we choose to walk on the path of obedience, which entails death to self and often includes suffering, God can be glorified and manifested through us. The Scriptures say,

> *For the earth will be filled with the knowledge of the glory of the* Lord, *as the waters cover the sea.* (Habakkuk 2:14)

The Lord promises us so much knowledge of His glory that the manifestations will fill the planet we inhabit. Extraordinary miracles that have never been seen before will begin to take place. Why? Because humanity is receiving the revealed knowledge of the glory of God. To know Jesus is to bring His reality, His dominion, His life, and His power to earth.

Prayer of Activation

Father of glory, we honor and worship You. Show us great and mighty things through the spirit of wisdom and revelation in the knowledge of You. Let us know all that You have for us in the new covenant You have made with us through Your Son Jesus. Impart to us the mysteries of the kingdom of God, so that we may increasingly serve You better. May Your kingdom come and Your will be done on earth as it is in heaven. In Jesus' name, amen!

Action Steps

♦ Write down ten things you have learned from the Scriptures or from biblical teaching about God's priorities for your life and for the world. Then, review them and begin to align your life with any of these priorities that you have not been giving much attention to. For example, you might pray about how you can minister to a widow or orphan spiritually and materially, and then follow the Spirit's leading in doing so. As you align your life with God's priorities, ask Him to give you revealed knowledge so that you can know more about His will for your life and obey it.

♦ On what are you setting your mind—things on earth or things above? Over the next week, evaluate what you spend much of your time thinking about and doing. Are you tempted to read gossip about celebrities? Are you spending the majority of your time on the pursuit of entertainment? Do you worry constantly? While rest, healthy recreation, and attending to our daily needs are necessary for everyone, if you are being distracted from what is important to God by trivial matters or excessive worrying, make a conscious decision to set your mind on things above through memorizing and meditating on God's Word. Begin by memorizing Scriptures related to a particular spiritual theme or by memorizing a chapter from a book in the New Testament. Memorize one or two verses every day, and then meditate on those verses during the following twenty-four hours, before you go on to the next verse or two.

EXPERIENCES WITH GOD'S GLORY

God Gives Supernatural Knowledge of an Assassination Plot

Pastor Jorge Pompa of Nuevo León, Mexico, was trained and equipped in the supernatural power of God, so that the gifts began to flow and growth began to manifest in his ministry. God led him into a new level of authority and dominion, and today, he has a congregation of 1,500.

Pastor Pompa attended sessions of the Supernatural Fivefold Ministry School at King Jesus Ministry, an event for the training of leaders and pastors. During this time, Pastor Guillermo Maldonado ministered and released boldness over the leadership through the Lord's Supper. When Pastor Pompa returned to his country, God showed him that there would be an assassination attempt on the mayor of the city, which would be carried out no later than February 24. Exercising the boldness he had received, he sent the mayor an urgent message asking for an appointment to see him. In his city, it is very difficult for a common citizen to meet with a mayor, but he was invited to come to the mayor's office.

When the pastor arrived at the appointed time, he said, "Sir, I am neither a nobody nor someone guided by emotion. I come to tell you that God said to me there will be an assassination attempt against you before the twenty-fourth of this month." The mayor stayed quiet and very serious, and the pastor warned him that the only way for God to save him would be for him to stop his witchcraft practices, because they were an abomination before God. The man bowed his head and began to cry. The pastor prayed for him and declared that he would not die. When he finished, the mayor confessed that he had received a death threat saying that if he did not leave the city before the twenty-fourth of February, they were going to kill him. He never had to leave! The power of God worked in his favor, and, to this day, God protects him and his family. Not only that, but Pastor Pompa's boldness also resulted in his being the first Christian pastor to receive the keys to the city.

A Passion to Seek God's Presence

"Lord, I have loved the habitation of Your house, and the place where Your glory dwells."
—Psalm 26:8

Introduction

A serious problem in the church today, especially in the United States, is that as people grow spiritually and are blessed by God, they become less aware of their need for Him—for His presence and power. We cannot hunger and thirst for something if we are unaware that we need it.

Some people have an intellectual desire to seek the presence of God, but they have no passion for it. This type of "desire" is a passive mental attitude; it is merely a wish or a yearning to reach something without any accompanying action to attain it. Passion, on the other hand, is a driving force, a spiritual energy, that shapes our lifestyles, mentalities, and actions. When a person is passionate about obtaining something, every thought and every ounce of his or her energy is dedicated to seeking and achieving that desired objective. Our mind-sets, our conversations, and our priorities are based on our hearts' true passions. Simple desire has never led anyone to accomplish anything. We need spiritual passion!

We cannot settle for just the initial encounter that we had with Jesus as our Savior; we must continually seek Him to have more encounters and experiences with Him and come to know Him more fully in all His various facets. We cannot be content with knowing *about* Him. We must know *Him*. Then, we can experience His wonderful love, grace, strength, and power. In this study, we will see how to develop a passion for God's presence, beginning with the examples of Moses, David, and Paul.

Study Questions

Part I: Moses' Longing for God's Presence

1. (a) When the Israelites witnessed the manifestations of God's presence on Mount Sinai, how did they react? (Exodus 20:18b)

    _____

    (b) What did the people then tell Moses regarding how they wanted to receive communications from God? Why? (Verse 19)

    _____

    _____

    (c) What did Moses tell them to encourage them to move nearer to God? (Verse 20)

    _____

    _____

    (d) While the people continued to "stand afar off," what did Moses do? (Verse 21)

    _____

2. (a) What did the Lord reply when Moses asked whom the Lord would send to help him lead the Israelites out of Egypt? (Exodus 33:14)

    _____

    (b) When Moses asked for God's presence to go with the entire nation of Israel, even though they'd been a *"stiff-necked people"* (Exodus 33:3, 5), what was the first thing God told him in response? (Verse 17a)

    _____

    (c) Why did God say He would do this? (Verse 17b)

    _____

3. (a) In what manner did the Lord speak to Moses? (Exodus 33:11a; Numbers 12:8a)

   _____

   (b) What reason did God give for speaking with Moses in this way? (Numbers 12:7b)

   _____

4. (a) For what reason did God allow the Israelites to hear His voice out of heaven and His words in the midst of the fire? (Deuteronomy 4:36a)

   _____

   (b) Why didn't God allow the people to see His form when He spoke to them from the midst of the fire? (Verse 16a)

   _____

   (c) In contrast to the corrupt, idolatrous desires of the people, what was Moses' pure desire? (Exodus 33:18)

   _____

Part II: David's Zeal for God

5. What was God's reason for choosing David to be king of Israel instead of Saul? Complete the following:

   1 Samuel 13:14: *"The LORD has sought for Himself* _____ _____ _____

   _____ _____ _____....*"*

6. (a) What did David say about the position he gave to God in his life? (Psalm 16:8a)

   _____

   (b) What had David discovered may be found in the presence of God and at His right hand? (Verse 11b)

   _____

7. What did David love? (Psalm 26:8)

   _____

8. (a) What *"one thing"* had David desired of the Lord, which he said he would seek? (Psalm 27:4a)

   _____

   (b) What two reasons did he give for desiring this? (Verse 4b)

   _____

   (c) How did David's heart respond when God said to him, *"Seek My face"*? (Verse 8)

   _____

**David was a man after God's own heart
because of his thirst and passion to seek His presence.**

---

9. (a) When did David say that he would seek God? (Psalm 63:1a)

   _____

   (b) How did he express his desire for God using a vivid metaphor? (Verse 1b)

   _____

   _____

   (c) Where did David look for God? (Verse 2a)

   _____

   (d) What did he want to see there? (Verse 2b)

   _____

(e) At what other time did David say he remembered God and meditated on Him? (Psalm 63:6)

_____

10. (a) When David took over as king of Israel, one of his first royal acts was to bring the ark—and, with it, the manifest presence of God—to Jerusalem, where he had established his residence and seat of government. What did David do in celebration as the ark was being transported to Jerusalem? (2 Samuel 6:14a)

_____

(b) How was this unreserved expression of joy in God described? Complete the following:

Verse 16b: "…*King David* [was] _____ _____

_____ *before the* LORD."

Part III: Paul's Intense Desire for Intimacy with Christ

11. What did Paul desire to know? (Philippians 3:10)

_____

_____

12. (a) What did Paul consider to be loss compared to the excellence of the knowledge of Christ Jesus his Lord? (Philippians 3:8a)

_____

(b) What reason did he give for counting these things *"as rubbish"*? Complete the following:

Verses 8b–9a: "…[I] *count them as rubbish,* _____ _____ _____

_____ _____ _____ ___ _____ _____

_____."

13. Paul showed his longing for the return of Jesus Christ, and for being in His presence, by the statements he made in relation to Christ's coming. Complete the following:

    (a) Philippians 3:20b: "...we also _____ _____ for the Savior, the Lord Jesus Christ."

    (b) 2 Timothy 4:8b: "...to all who have _____ _____ _____."

14. What did Paul want the Ephesians (and all believers) to comprehend concerning God's love, as he had evidently experienced in communion with Him? (Ephesians 3:18b)

    _____

REFLECTIONS ON KNOWING GOD

In the original languages of the Bible, there are several words that were used for the verb "to know." *Gnosis*—a Greek word that alludes to informative, mental, theoretical, and scientific knowledge. *Epignosis*—a Greek word that indicates experimental knowledge or knowledge acquired by practice or experience; at the personal level, it refers to having intimacy with another individual or knowing that person intimately. *Yada*—a Hebrew word that means to have intimate knowledge of or to know someone at the intimate level. The will of God is for every believer to have experiences of Him—intimate, face-to-face encounters with Him. What Paul was expressing in Ephesians 3:18–19 ("*to know the love of Christ*") is that we should reach the *epignosis*, the love of Christ that exceeds all *gnosis*.

Part IV: Thirsting for God

15. (a) As a review, what kind of "*cisterns*" had God's people hewn for themselves instead of relying on God? (Jeremiah 2:13b)

    _____

(b) What kind of fountain did the Lord call Himself, whom the Israelites had forsaken? (Jeremiah 2:13a)

_____

16. (a) For whom did the psalmist thirst? (Psalm 42:2a)

_____

(b) How did the psalmist express his spiritual thirst to God? (Verse 1a)

_____

17. What did Jesus say we should do if we are spiritually thirsty? Complete the following:

John 7:37b: *"If anyone thirsts, _____ _____ _____ _____*

_____ _____ _____."

18. (a) What will occur in the lives of those who believe in Jesus? (John 7:38b)

_____

(b) To whom was Jesus referring with this metaphor? (Verse 39)

_____

Part V: A Passion for God Leads to Revealed Knowledge

19. (a) What kind of a man was Simeon? (Luke 2:25a)

_____

(b) What had he been waiting for? (Verse 25b)

_____

(c) Who was upon Simeon? (Verse 25b)

_____

(d) What had the Holy Spirit revealed to him? (Luke 2:26)

_____

(e) By whose direction did Simeon go into the temple? (Verse 27a)

_____

(f) After Simeon had recognized the infant Jesus as the Messiah, taken Him in his arms, and blessed God, with what words did he affirm that God had fulfilled the revelation He had given him? (Verse 29)

_____

20. (a) How is Zacchaeus described? (Luke 19:2b)

_____

(b) In his yearning to see who Jesus was, what did Zacchaeus do, since he was short? (Verse 4)

_____

(c) What did Jesus tell Zacchaeus when He saw him in the tree? (Verse 5)

_____

(d) After Zacchaeus received the revelation of who Jesus was and repented of his sin, what did Jesus say to some skeptical onlookers? Complete the following:

Verse 9: "Today _____ _____ _____ _____

_____ _____, _because he also is a son of Abraham._"

(e) Jesus told Zacchaeus that He must stay at his house that day. To what might He have been referring in a spiritual sense, a truth we looked at in the previous study? (John 14:23)

_____

_____

Being aware of our need for the presence of God keeps us hungry and thirsty for it.

---

21. (a) The Samaritan woman at the well came into the presence of Jesus, and this led her to develop a greater thirst for God. What did Jesus tell her about what will result for the person who drinks the water He gives? (John 4:14a)

    _____

    (b) What will the water become in him? (Verse 14b)

    _____

    (c) What deep truths about God and His true worshippers did Jesus express to the Samaritan woman when she inquired about the correct way to worship? (Verse 24)

    _____

    _____

A hunger and thirst for God activates His provision.
He will not manifest where there is no need.

Part VI: Develop a Passion for God

22. In what way can we show our passion for God? (Matthew 22:37)

    _____

23. On what can we build our love for God? (1 John 4:19)

    _____

24. (a) With what kind of love has God loved His people? (Jeremiah 31:3a)

    _____

(b) What action has He taken toward His people because of this love? (Jeremiah 31:3b)

_____

25. (a) With loving but firm chastisement, what did God tell the Laodicean church He would do because of their lukewarm spiritual state, or their lack of passion for Him and His ways? (Revelation 3:16 NIV)

_____

(b) What did He tell them to do in response to His chastening? (Verse 19b)

_____

(c) How did David describe the Lord's attitude toward His people? (Psalm 103:8)

_____

26. (a) When are we encouraged to seek the Lord and to call upon Him? (Isaiah 55:6)

_____

(b) What will God do when we repent and turn to Him? (Verse 7b)

_____

27. (a) What did the psalmist pray that sums up his passion for God? (Psalm 73:25)

_____

_____

(b) Even when our flesh and our heart fail, what will God be for us? (Verse 26)

_____

The key to getting something you really want is to be willing to risk anything to get it.

Conclusion

We must ask the Holy Spirit to give us the desire and thirst for God's water of life. When we are baptized with the Holy Spirit, with the evidence of speaking in other tongues, rivers of living water will begin to flow in us. Yet baptism with the Holy Spirit is only the initial infilling by which we experience the supernatural power and life of the Holy Spirit. Afterwards, we must seek to be continually filled. This filling enables us to walk in the Spirit at all times—for the long run. Otherwise, we will dry up, regardless of how great and powerful that first infilling was. We should never stop seeking to be filled by the Holy Spirit.

Moreover, it is also not enough to be touched by the Holy Spirit or to receive a blessing from Him ourselves. Once our thirst has been quenched, we can pray for the sick, testify of Jesus, and become effective instruments of God that will bless many other people. But, to maintain these ministries, we must keep returning to Jesus to "drink."

Strangely, when believers do seek God, continually returning to drink of His living water through fasting, prayer, worship, and intercession, they are often regarded as fanatics. Yet many of these seekers understand that multitudes of people in the world are lost, and they desire to help them. They know that some people are trapped in addiction, some are confused, some are despairing, some are suffering from broken homes, and some are on the verge of committing suicide. They need to receive a revelation of hope and restoration, and they can do so through our witness as we are continually filled with the Holy Spirit and with power.

Prayer of Activation

Father of glory, our greatest desire is for You. Like David, we set You always before us. We commit to seeking Your face. Our souls thirst for You, as in a dry and thirsty land. Quench our thirst with Your living water. May it flow out of our hearts to bring salvation, healing, and deliverance to the multitudes who need You. In the name of Jesus, amen.

Action Steps

+ If you have only a remote desire to seek God but want to exchange it for true passion, pray that the Holy Spirit would descend upon you with His fire and fill you with His passion. Ask God to free you from spiritual lethargy and to ignite within you a flame of spiritual love and zeal for Him.

+ A passion for God usually begins with a commitment—not a feeling. And it is maintained by a continual renewal of that commitment. Make the decision to meet with

God every day in a quiet place, free of distractions. Pour out your heart before Him, praise Him for what He has done in your life, and then wait quietly in His presence in a spirit of worship. As you do this each day, with sincerity and the knowledge that God's Spirit will help you in your human weakness, then your passion for God, your loving heavenly Father, will continue to grow.

EXPERIENCES WITH GOD'S GLORY

Signs and Wonders in the Middle of the Peruvian Jungle

A few years ago, Pastor Guillermo Maldonado ministered to thousands of pastors and other church leaders in Trujillo, Peru. During the conference, he kept seeing a flag in one section of the meeting place that read, "Sons of the kingdom in the Peruvian jungle." That section was the most boisterous in their praise; they danced and jumped nonstop! After the service, they asked to speak with Pastor Maldonado, so they met in the hotel where he was staying. What he heard from them moved him beyond words.

In the middle of the Peruvian jungle, where there are minimal economic resources, and where medical care is scarce, these people were mounting a spiritual revolution. The group had traveled over twenty-four hours by land to get to Trujillo for the opportunity to request spiritual covering by King Jesus Ministry. They explained how hard they'd had to work to gather enough money to buy the ministry's materials, which were helping to transform lives. People were being liberated from religiosity. The practice of praise had been revolutionized in their churches. They had learned to hear the voice of God. They were radical, and the signs of the believer followed them! They found drug addicts where they are hiding, led them to Christ, and delivered them. They ministered healing to the sick and deliverance to the demon possessed. The hospitals had sent them their hopeless cases. Their hunger and thirst for God and for His power were releasing His hand of justice in their favor.

One of their pastors, Benito Risco, shared specific testimonies of what God was doing in the Peruvian jungle. A mayor in his area had skin cancer, to the degree that when he would lie down, his skin would peel off on his clothes. His body was one great boil. He had used up all of his resources seeking a cure, but the doctors had given him no hope of recovery. Pastor Benito and his people shared the gospel with him, and he received Jesus into his heart and attended a deliverance retreat, where he was freed from unforgiveness, among other things. The following week, he noticed his skin looked new. Where there had been one boil after the other, now he had normal, healthy skin. Jesus had completely healed him! The doctors could not explain what had happened.

In another case, a twenty-three-year-old man who was in the last stage of AIDS had been sent home from the hospital to die and was suffering with convulsions. Pastor Benito visited this young man, led him to Christ, and prayed for healing, and the young man felt a little better. They returned two more times to pray for him. Today, this young man is completely healed!

Pastor Benito oversees thirty churches with over five thousand believers—in the middle of the jungle. They are producing great fruit, manifesting miracles and signs. Even though they had suffered persecution for manifesting the power of Jesus, they chose to obey the voice of God because they wanted to see people saved and to provide answers to their needs. Their thirst for God keeps them seeking more and more of Him, and signs follow them!

Study 10

Conditions, Rewards, and Benefits of the Glory

"If My people who are called by My name will humble themselves, and pray and seek My face, and turn from their wicked ways, then I will hear from heaven, and will forgive their sin and heal their land."
—2 Chronicles 7:14

Introduction

A passion for God is foundational for experiencing His glory. Besides what we learned in the previous study, an essential way to develop this passion is to recognize and fulfill four spiritual conditions for receiving God's rewards and benefits. These are the same conditions God required of the Israelites to receive His blessings, and the same conditions He places on us for His justice, revival, and glory to descend on our cities and nations. If we will meet these conditions, three wonderful rewards and benefits will take place as God establishes and expands His kingdom on earth. Let us now explore the conditions, rewards, and benefits of the glory.

Study Questions

Part I: Four Conditions for Receiving God's Blessings

1. What is the first condition God gave His people for receiving the blessings of His glory? (2 Chronicles 7:14a)

_____

2. Similarly, what did Jesus say is required if we are to enter the kingdom of heaven? (Matthew 18:3)

   _____

3. What will God do if we humble ourselves in His sight? (James 4:10)

   _____

4 What is the second condition God gave His people for receiving the blessings of His glory? Complete the following:

   2 Chronicles 7:14a: *"If My people…will humble themselves, and* _____*…."*

5. What did God say He would do if His people returned to Him? (Zechariah 1:3)

   _____

6. What do we need to assist us with our prayers? Complete the following:

   Zechariah 12:10: *"And I will pour on the house of David and on the inhabitants of*

   Jerusalem _____ _____ _____ _____ _____

   _____*."*

7. How does the Holy Spirit help us to pray as we ought to? (Romans 8:26b, 27b)

   _____

   _____

8. What did James say about the *"effective, fervent prayer of a righteous man"*? (James 5:16b)

   _____

9. What is the third condition God gave His people for receiving the blessings of His glory? (2 Chronicles 7:14a)

_____

10. What did God say would happen if His people searched for Him with all their hearts? (Jeremiah 29:13)

_____

11. To review, what is the ultimate result of our search, which is equivalent to eternal life? (John 17:3b)

_____

12. What is the fourth condition God gave His people for receiving the blessings of His glory? (2 Chronicles 7:14a)

_____

13. (a) In what shall we be saved? (Isaiah 30:15a)

_____

(b) What does godly sorrow produce? (2 Corinthians 7:10a)

_____

(c) What does worldly sorrow produce? (Verse 10b)

_____

14. Paraphrase the practical instruction John the Baptist gave to the following groups to help them understand how to *"bear fruits worthy of repentance"* (Luke 3:8).

(a) The people: (Luke 3:11)

_____

_____

(b) The tax collectors: (Luke 3:13)

_____

(c) The soldiers: (Verse 14)

_____

_____

15. (a) What did Jesus tell the believers at the church in Ephesus that they had left? (Revelation 2:4b)

_____

(b) What did He tell them to do in order to remedy this situation? (Verse 5a)

_____

Part II: Three Results of Seeking God

16. What is God called in relation to those who diligently seek Him? Complete the following:

Hebrews 11:6b: *"He is _____ _____ of those who diligently seek Him."*

17. What did God tell His people would be the first result if they met the conditions for receiving the blessings of His glory? (2 Chronicles 7:14b)

_____

18. (a) What reason did the psalmist give for loving the Lord? (Psalm 116:1)

_____

(b) Why did he say he would call upon the Lord as long as he lived? (Verse 2)

_____

19. (a) What confidence can we have in God in relation to our prayers? (1 John 5:14)

_____

(b) What do we know, based on the assurance that God hears us? (Verse 15)

_____

20. What did God tell His people would be the second result if they met the conditions for receiving the blessings of His glory? (2 Chronicles 7:14b)

_____

21. What assurance of forgiveness do the Scriptures give us, if we have confessed our sins to God? (1 John 1:9)

_____

22. How far from us has God removed our transgressions? (Psalm 103:12)

_____

23. What did God tell His people would be the third result if they met the conditions for receiving the blessings of His glory? (2 Chronicles 7:14b)

_____

REFLECTIONS ON "LAND"

"Land" in 2 Chronicles 7:14 represents one's personal life, family, ministry, job or business, community, and nation. In each of these areas, there is a great need for human beings to have a personal encounter with God. People yearn for healing in their bodies and souls, but they also want financial and spiritual prosperity. God wants to heal our "land" and end the consequences of sin and separation from Him: confusion and lack of direction, frustration, depression, discord, injustice, drug addiction, the shedding of innocent blood, and much more. However, the healing will not take place until we humble ourselves, pray, seek His presence, and walk away from wickedness and ungodliness.

24. What won't those who seek the Lord lack? (Psalm 34:10b)

_____

25. List various ways in which God blessed David. (Psalm 103:3–5)

_____

_____

_____

Part III: We Must Seek God's Glory "Until..."

26. (a) As we seek the Lord and turn from our wicked ways, what must we "sow" for ourselves, and what must we "break up"? (Hosea 10:12a)

_____

(b) In what must we reap? (Verse 12a)

_____

(c) What word in Hosea 10:12 (NIV) indicates that seeking the Lord may take perseverance? Complete the following:

Verse 12b (NIV): "For it is time to seek the LORD _____ he comes...."

(d) What will be the result when we sow righteousness and break up our fallow ground? (Verse 12b)

_____

27. Jesus encouraged us to go to God in three ways, each one with a specific result. Record His instructions below. (Matthew 7:7)

_____

_____

_____

28. In what manner did King Hezekiah seek God, so that his prosperity was the result? (2 Chronicles 31:21b)

_____

REFLECTIONS ON PROSPERITY

The word "prospered" in 2 Chronicles 31:21 is translated from the Hebrew word *tsalach*, and among its meanings are "to advance," "to make progress," "to succeed," or "to be profitable." Prosperity is always connected to seeking God's presence because prosperity is more than financial stability—that is only a very small part of it. Prosperity goes hand in hand with being able to do the will of God, having life in our spirits, and enjoying health in body and soul. When we passionately seek the glory, or the manifest presence of God, He releases His favor and grace upon us, which leads to the provision of all our needs. Furthermore, we are equipped to carry the same blessings to our circle of influence.

29. What will happen if we don't grow weary and lose heart while doing good? (Galatians 6:9)

_____

If we have yet to experience a breakthrough in an area where we need one, it could be that we lack hunger and thirst for God.

Conclusion

It is time to pray for an outpouring of the Holy Spirit, for revival, and for the manifestation of the glory of God, so that our lives, families, ministries, cities, and nations can be transformed. God is seeking people who are committed to make themselves available to Him as vessels through which He heals and delivers.

In my experience, people who truly seek God do not lack anything. God is faithful to keep His Word. We should continue to work and to care for our families, but let us seek God first, because He is our true Provider. We may experience moments in which things do not work out the way we want them to—in our finances, our health, or other life circumstances—but these situations are only temporary. In the end, God will work all things out in our favor. (See Romans 8:28.)

We can seek God in various ways, including through worship, fasting, and prayer. Prayer with a sense of desperation and urgency must be made *until* God shows His mercy. What is God waiting for? He waits for you and me to cry out in utter dependency, like a drowning man, "Help me!" God is waiting for His people to come to this point. Seek His face *until* His glory—His presence—manifests!

Prayer of Activation

Father of glory, pour out Your Spirit of grace and supplication upon us. We desire to fully humble ourselves, seek Your face, and turn from our wicked ways, bearing fruit worthy of true repentance. Hear our prayer, forgive our sin, and heal our land—our nations and all aspects of our lives. Rain Your righteousness on us, for Your glory. In Jesus' name, amen.

Action Steps

+ Humble yourself: Confess any known sins to the Lord and ask Him to cleanse you of underlying attitudes and thoughts that do not honor Him, which you may not be aware of.

+ Pray: Pray with your understanding and pray in the Spirit (see 1 Corinthians 14:15) for yourself, your family, your community, your nation, and the world, asking that God's kingdom would come and His will would be done on earth as it is in heaven.

+ Seek God's face: Spend time in the presence of God with no other purpose but to praise and worship Him and deepen your love for Him. Read His Word with a re-newed commitment to conforming to the image of Christ.

+ Turn from your wicked ways: Begin anew to obey and serve God wholeheartedly, setting aside the things that would keep you from loving and following Him as you should.

EXPERIENCES WITH GOD'S GLORY

Deliverance from Drugs, Alcohol, and Sexual Perversion

A young lady named Jennifer had been rebellious and a drug user, and she had prac-ticed a lesbian lifestyle since the second grade. After she turned eleven, her parents began to purchase marijuana and alcohol for her. She was addicted to the drug Xanax at age thirteen and to cocaine at fifteen. Her parents gave up trying to discipline her and simply threw her out of the house, so she became homeless. At sixteen, she used heroin, until the morning she woke up in a place she did not recognize and realized that she had been raped.

Jennifer's life had been a disaster for as long as she could remember. She could not get through one day without drugs, alcohol, or sexual perversion. She also suffered from bulimia. One day, tired of living and on the verge of ending her life, she visited King Jesus Ministry, and the presence of God touched her. She threw herself on the altar and surrendered to Him, and her life began to change. She used to hate her parents, but now she loves them. She was delivered from bitterness, from the shame of her lesbian lifestyle, and from depression. She had actually tried to end her drug addiction by leaving the drugs on the altar several times, but, each time, she returned to the world and to her old habits. This vicious cycle continued until, one day, she came back to the church with all her "baggage" and said, "I will never return to that life." She became a new person and has never looked back. Today, she is a leader in the House of Peace [the church's home fellowship ministry] and a mentor in the church.

It is easy to see the hand of God upon Jennifer's life and realize that God delivers, heals, and protects us from the world. The love and power of God transformed this young woman on both the inside and the outside when she surrendered wholeheartedly to Him. Nothing and no one else—not psychology, medical treatments, or her parents—can take credit for her new life. It was accomplished solely by the presence and power of God.

Study 11
Transformed into His Glory

"But we all, with unveiled face, beholding as in a mirror the glory of the Lord, are being transformed into the same image from glory to glory, just as by the Spirit of the Lord."
—2 Corinthians 3:18

Introduction

We do not change into the likeness of Jesus because we are disciplined people who pray a lot, give tithes, and attend church every week. All these things are good, and we should continue to practice them. However, what really changes us is seeing God face-to-face in His manifest glory!

Many people resist transformation because they have conformed to the world. They are in bondage to man-made traditions and are afraid of change because they believe it could affect their position, status, respectability, finances, or other aspects of their life. On the other hand, they are also greatly dissatisfied because they know God has something more for them, but they do not know how to define or describe it, much less reach it.

We must seek to be transformed as we spend time in the presence of God—through private and corporate worship and by reading and meditating on His Word—all which continually make us into His image. We can no longer stay the same. When we enter into God's presence, we will be changed and ignited with spiritual passion to do the work of spreading His kingdom throughout the world.

Study Questions

Part I: From Glory to Glory

1. How does the book of Proverbs describe the *"path of the just ["righteous" NIV]"*? (Proverbs 4:18)

   _____

   _____

2. (a) As we behold the glory of the Lord *"as in a mirror,"* what happens to us? (2 Corinthians 3:18b)

    _____

    (b) Who effects this change in us? (Verse 18b)

    _____

    (c) What may be found where the Spirit of the Lord is? (Verse 17b)

    _____

    (d) What word in the verse below indicates that our transformation into the image of Christ is an ongoing process? Complete the following:

    1 Corinthians 3:18a: *"We are _____ transformed into the same image from glory to glory...."*

**What changes a person is not time spent in church,
as such, but time spent in God's presence.**

KEY DEFINITION: *"Liberty"* in 2 Corinthians 3:17 is translated from the Greek word *eleutheria*, which means "freedom without restrictions, regulations, norms, laws, or traditions." The freedom we receive from the Holy Spirit is not the freedom to do as we please. Rather, it empowers us to do the right thing in the presence of God.

---

3. For what purpose was Christ made to *"be sin"* for us? (2 Corinthians 5:21b)

    _____

4. (a) What did the apostle Paul *"press on"* to lay hold of? (Philippians 3:12b)

    _____

(b) In doing so, what did he purposefully "forget," and what did he "reach forward" to? (Philippians 3:13)

_____

_____

(c) What did he *"press toward"*? (Verse 14)

_____

5. (a) What are we to "lay aside" in order to run the spiritual race that is set before us? (Hebrews 12:1b)

_____

(b) Whom must we focus on in order to reach the finish line? (Verse 2a)

_____

Part II: Renewal and Transformation

6. (a) What is one means by which we are transformed into the image of Christ? (Romans 12:2a)

_____

(b) What does this process enable us to *"prove"*? (Verse 2b)

_____

No transformation is permanent until the mind has been renewed.

REFLECTIONS ON TRANSFORMATION

The Greek word translated *"transfigured"* (Matthew 17:2) in relation to Jesus' transfiguration is the same word used in Romans 12:2 for *"transformed"*: *"Be transformed by the renewing of your mind."* That word is *metamorphoo*, and it means "to change into another form," "to transform," or "to transfigure." The main idea of the verb is to die to one form of life in order to be born into another. When Jesus was transfigured, He reflected the reality of the world to come and manifested His glory. The disciples had seen Him live and walk under the anointing, but on that day, for the first time, they saw His true glory—the glory He had left behind when He came to the world. And, as we renew our minds according to His nature, we will reflect the reality of His glory. The Word says we are *"transformed...from glory to glory"* (2 Corinthians 3:18). This truth enables us to understand that we are transformed from "one place to another," or that we advance from one dimension to another. If we want to move with the glory of God, we cannot do so with a mentality of settling down in one place and of having "arrived." Rather, we are to have a mind-set of constant movement, so we can go from one dimension of glory to another.

The renewed mind is the essential tool needed to bring the reality of the kingdom, the power, and the glory to earth.

---

7. What aren't we to be conformed to? (Romans 12:2a)

   _____

8. What did Peter say to the religious officials who wanted the apostles to conform to their way of thinking, which was contrary to God's? (Acts 5:29b)

   _____

9. What did Paul say he would not be, if he still desired to please men? (Galatians 1:10b)

   _____

KEY DEFINITION: The Greek word for *"conformed"* in Romans 12:2 is *suschematizo*. This term comes from two root words: *sun*, which means "with," and *schema*, which means "figure," "form," "shape," "appearance," or "external condition." Thus, "to be conformed" refers to adaptation and accommodation, or taking the form, shape, or appearance of the pattern of this world. *Suschematizo* highlights a change in external—not internal—appearance. Sometimes, this term is translated as "disguise." The idea here is that the world is pushing to give us form according to its pattern, similar to wearing new shoes that rub against the natural shape of our feet—giving us an external and transitory appearance that does not transform us from within. It does not remove sin, depression, or bitterness, nor does it give abundant life. In essence, what the world gives is only a disguise; it is not what we are meant to be or can be in Christ.

When we conform to someone or something, we stop being transformed.

---

10. (a) Those who are born again have *"put off the old man"* (Colossians 3:9) of sin and have *"put on the new man"* (verse 10). In what way is the new man renewed? (Verse 10b)

_____

(b) What specific qualities are we to *"put on"* in relation to the new man? (Verse 12)

_____

(c) How should we conduct ourselves in relation to others? (Verse 13)

_____

(d) What is the most important thing we need to *"put on,"* which Paul called the *"bond of perfection"*? (Verse 14)

_____

11. (a) What is continually happening to the *"inward man"* of believers, despite the fact that their physical bodies are growing weaker and *"perishing"*? (2 Corinthians 4:16)

_____

(b) What can an affliction in our lives "work" for us, if we respond to it with faith and hope in God? (Verse 17b)

_____

12. (a) What character trait does tribulation produce in our lives, if we allow it to? (Romans 5:3b)

_____

(b) What other qualities are produced as a result? (Verse 4)

_____

(c) How are we to respond to our tribulations? (Verse 3a)

_____

(d) What must we avoid doing in the face of trials and persecutions, something God takes no pleasure in? (Hebrews 10:38b)

_____

13. (a) If we are persecuted for the name of Christ, what rests upon us? (1 Peter 4:14a)

_____

(b) As a result, what occurs on behalf of Christ, on our part? (Verse 14b)

_____

Part III: Obstacles to Godly Transformation

14. What are two main obstacles to godly transformation, which the prophet Samuel included in his reprimand of King Saul? Complete the following:

1 Samuel 15:23: "For _____ is as the sin of witchcraft, and _____ is as iniquity and idolatry."

15. What are we warned not to do when we hear God's voice? (Hebrews 3:8a, 15b)

_____

Rebellion says, "I will not do it," while stubbornness says, "I will do it my way."

16. (a) Following the exodus from Egypt, what did the *"stubborn and rebellious generation"* of Israelites fail to "set aright"? (Psalm 78:8b)

    _____

    (b) What deficiency was in the spirit of that generation? (Verse 8b)

    _____

17. What do we need to have in order to begin receiving wisdom and instruction from God? Complete the following:

    Proverbs 1:7a: "_____ _____ _____ _____ _____ *is the*

    beginning of knowledge…."

18. Another obstacle to godly transformation is the same sin for which the devil was condemned. What is that sin? (1 Timothy 3:6)

    _____

19. (a) List various negative outcomes of this sin. (Proverbs 11:2a; 13:10a; 29:23; 16:18)

    _____

    (b) List some blessings the humble receive. (Psalm 147:6a; 149:4b; Proverbs 11:2b; 29:23b; Matthew 18:4; 23:12; James 4:6b)

    _____

    _____

A generation that does not embrace change will not impact the world.

---

20. (a) How does God respond to those who are proud? (1 Peter 5:5b)

    _____

(b) What does He give to those who are humble? (1 Peter 5:5b)

_____

(c) What will God do for those who humble themselves under His mighty hand? (Verse 6b)

_____

21. A third obstacle to godly transformation is to deny the need for change in one's life.

(a) If we say that we have no sin, what do we do to ourselves? (1 John 1:8a)

_____

(b) As a consequence, what key component of spiritual life is not in us? (Verse 8b)

_____

(c) If we claim we have not sinned, what do we imply about God? (Verse 10a NIV)

_____

(d) As a consequence, what key component of spiritual life has no place in our lives? (Verse 10b)

_____

The glory of God, or His presence, exposes the spiritual condition of an individual.

22. (a) In study 9, we discussed the lukewarm spiritual state of the Christians of the church at Laodicea, who were reprimanded by the risen Christ in the book of Revelation. What did the Laodiceans say about themselves that showed they didn't sense a need for spiritual transformation? (Revelation 3:17a)

_____

(b) What was their true spiritual state, of which they were unaware? (Verse 17b)

_____

23. What counsel should we heed, in order to avoid being presumptuous like the Laodiceans? (Proverbs 3:7)

_____

REFLECTIONS ON WHAT THE GLORY RELEASES

The glory of God releases something in the hearts of people that cannot be received directly through hearing teachings, reading books, listening to messages on CD, or receiving an anointing through the laying on of hands—even though these things are good and can point us to the glory. What the glory of God releases can be received only in His presence; there, people's vision is enlarged, and a passion for expanding the kingdom and winning souls is ignited within them. The glory of God releases empathy and love for others, as it generates zeal to do His will. Above all, a thirst for seeking the face of God and knowing Him intimately increases exponentially in people. If we sincerely want to be changed and transformed, we must dare to enter into His presence and stay in His movement, from glory to glory, without stopping or becoming stagnant.

24. A fourth obstacle to godly transformation is having a spirit of "religion" and legalism.

    (a) Instead of living in their newfound freedom in Christ, what were the Colossians subjecting themselves to? (Colossians 2:20b)

    _____

    (b) On what were the regulations based? (Verse 22b)

    _____

    (c) What did these regulations have an appearance of? Complete the following:

    Verse 23a: _"These things indeed have an appearance of _____ _____

    _____ _____, _____

    _____, and _____ _____ _____

    _____...."_

(d) How useful were the regulations in overcoming the fleshly nature? (Colossians 2:23b)

_____

When Christians cease to be changed,
they lose their power and return to religion and formality.

---

25. (a) What did the Lord say about the Israelites, who had fallen into religion and legalism? (Isaiah 29:13a)

_____

_____

(b) What was the faulty foundation of their instruction on the "fear," or reverence, of the Lord? (Verse 13b)

_____

The greatest tragedy in life is to lose the presence of God and not even know it.

---

26. (a) By what—and through what—are we saved, if not by religion? (Ephesians 2:8a)

_____

(b) What two things is salvation *not* a result of? (Verses 8b–9a)

_____

(c) How does salvation come to us? (Verse 8b)

_____

27. What has Christ done to the "*handwriting of requirements that was against us,*" since we have all failed to obey the holy law of God in our own strength and abilities? (Colossians 2:14)

_____

_____

28. False religion, having only a "*form of godliness,*" often shows its counterfeit nature by what it "denies." Complete the following:

    2 Timothy 3:5: "*…having a form of godliness but* _____ _____

    _____."

29. Recall in what way the Lord confirmed the reality of the apostles' preaching. (Mark 16:20b)

_____

_____

Without the manifestations of the supernatural power of God, Christianity is like any other religion.

Part IV: The Final Transformation in Glory

30. (a) What will happen "*in a moment, in the twinkling of an eye*" to believers who have died, and to believers who are alive, when Christ returns? (1 Corinthians 15:52b)

_____

_____

    (b) What will be the nature of the change that will occur for all believers? (Verse 53)

_____

_____

31. What transformation will take place in its fullness when Jesus is revealed, and we *"see Him as He is"*? (1 John 3:2b)

_____

32. What analogy did Peter use to describe how, in the *"power and coming of our Lord Jesus Christ"* (2 Peter 1:16), we will be completely transformed into His likeness? Complete the following:

2 Peter 1:19b: *"…until* _____ _____ _____ _____ _____

_____ _____ _____ _____

_____ _____."

Conclusion

Since we need to be continually transformed from glory to glory, there is a problem when we are not in the process of being changed—it means we do not currently walk in the glory of God. This is the reason for the lack of transformation we observe in the lives of many believers: they are not being regularly exposed to the glory of the Father.

Surely, no change is easy; it is usually difficult and painful. But if that is what it takes to enter into a greater dimension of God's glory, we need it. Are you willing to be transformed? If your answer is yes, God will take care of everything because He does not want you to waste your time following religious norms. He wants you to enjoy the highest dimension of His glory.

Moreover, being in the glory is not just an "experience" for us to bask in; it brings about a transformation that allows us to minister to others in remarkable ways. Jesus came to earth to show us how to reach out to others with salvation, healing, and deliverance, just as He did. Let us be transformed into His image *"in ever increasing splendor"* (2 Corinthians 3:18 AMP).

Prayer of Activation

Father of glory, fill us once again with Your Holy Spirit, so that we may be like the sun that *"shines ever brighter unto the perfect day."* Impart to us the knowledge of You, enabling us to be renewed in that knowledge every day according to the image of Christ in His glory. In Jesus' name, amen.

Action Steps

- Ask yourself these questions: Since I became a Christian, have I remained the same, or have I been growing more like Christ? Have I stopped being transformed? Why? Are the power and presence of God active in my life? If not, when did the life of the supernatural diminish for me? Have I become irrelevant in the advancement of the kingdom of God? When did the services at my church seem to become routine? Have I conformed myself to my worldly surroundings or to my sickness, poverty, or sin? Answer each of these questions honestly. God calls every believer to change because He wants to take us to another level in Him. Ask Him to deliver you from everything negative to which you have conformed, so that the Holy Spirit can begin to transform your life, your family, and your ministry, starting within you.

- Make a decision not to dwell on your past failures or to become self-satisfied with your past successes. Seek to develop the attitude of Paul: *"Forgetting those things which are behind and reaching forward to those things which are ahead, I press toward the goal for the prize of the upward call of God in Christ Jesus"* (Philippians 3:13–14).

EXPERIENCES WITH GOD'S GLORY

Deliverances from Fear, Depression, and Hatred

A young man was terribly afraid of failure and had never had a vision and direction for his life. He had grown up without a father, and although his mother had tried to fill the void in his heart, she had been unable to because she, also, was in great pain. Her divorce had led to years of depression, a condition that she had passed on to her son. The young man said, "I suffered with depression for over twenty-nine years. I had no faith in myself and felt abandoned and rejected. I felt I had no future or plans. My life was sedentary. My thinking was limited, and I had no interests or aspirations."

This young man came to King Jesus Ministry one Sunday when Pastor Guillermo Maldonado was preaching on the spirit of fear and the boldness we need in order to take action and be brave, and the message impacted him. When the pastor finished speaking, he ministered deliverance from the spirit of fear and imparted the boldness of the Spirit. The young man testified that, since that day, his life has been completely transformed. He used to think he would have to deal with depression for the rest of his life, but now he dares to do things he had never imagined being capable of doing. The perfect love of God cast out all fear from his heart.

In another testimony, a young man had grown up with disappointment, resentment, and much anger toward his father due to his psychological, physical, and verbal abuse of his mother. His hatred toward his father became so strong that he decided to kill him. He found a knife, sharpened it, and then waited for his father to provoke him. But someone else killed his father before he had the opportunity to do so. Losing his father in that way led to increased disappointment, guilt, and pain, as well as to additional anger because he had not been able to kill his father. His heart had been corrupted by hate and vengeance.

In addition, everything that had happened to him in his youth had led to his involvement with gangs. While he was a gang member, he used drugs, and his life went from bad to worse. Then, this broken young man visited King Jesus Ministry, went to the altar, received Jesus, had an encounter with the presence of God, and was transformed. He attended the ministry's retreat for inner healing and deliverance for new believers. During the retreat, the presence of God touched him, and he cried like a child. A leader ministered deliverance, and he was freed from guilt, resentment, and pain. He forgave his father, and now he is completely free! The root of bitterness was removed from his heart, and he can now enjoy life.

Study 12

CREATING AN ATMOSPHERE TO BRING HIS PRESENCE, PART 1

"Whoever offers praise glorifies [God]."
—Psalm 50:23

Introduction

When people are not worshipping God in spirit and truth on a continual basis, they are unable to create the environment to bring His presence. We must learn how to invite a spiritual atmosphere of worship for the glory to manifest and for miracles, signs, and wonders to take place. In doing so, we will be what the Bible calls *"true worshippers"* (John 4:23)—something that cannot be accomplished by just singing well. True worshippers are those who have had a revelation of genuine worship.

Through praise and worship, we welcome our Lord and King into our midst. If we want to produce truly deep and heartfelt worship, we often need to first ascend in vibrant, loud, and powerful praise. Then, it is important to discern when the spirit of praise has receded in order to allow the spirit of worship to lead. Our praise and worship should be carried out in accordance with the One whom we desire to please—God Himself. That is the only way to follow the leading of the Spirit and avoid getting lost in our human efforts.

In this study, we will explore aspects of praise, so that we may begin to gain an understanding of how to create an atmosphere to bring God's presence. Then, in the next study, we will investigate the topic of worship.

Study Questions

Part I: The Lord Deserves Our Praise and Worship

1. What is God worthy to receive, and why? (Revelation 4:11)

   _____

   _____

2. Psalm 24, which describes *"gates"* and *"everlasting doors"* being lifted up to allow the *"King of glory"* entrance (see verses 7, 9), may be considered a metaphor for how we are to welcome God into our midst through praise. How is the King of glory described? (Verse 8b)

   _____

3. (a) Where did David say the holy God is *"enthroned"*? (Psalm 22:3b)

   _____

   (b) When a person offers praise to God, what does he do? (Psalm 50:23a)

   _____

A hard spiritual atmosphere may be the result of poor praise and worship.

---

4. (a) In what manner are we to praise the Lord, as David did? (Psalm 138:1a)

   _____

   (b) When is an appropriate time to praise the Lord? (Psalm 113:3a; 34:1)

   _____

<u>KEY DEFINITIONS</u>: Praise is an exuberant, clamorous, enthusiastic expression that often includes many words and a physical display. Worship involves fewer words—at times, no words are needed at all and there is total silence, because it has more to do with inwardly pouring out our hearts before God and asking Him to manifest His sovereign presence.

Part II: Expressions of Praise

5. Praise to the Lord may be expressed in various ways. List two of these ways. (Psalm 66:1a, 2a)

   _____

6. (a) What types of songs did the apostle Paul encourage the New Testament believers to "speak" to one another? (Ephesians 5:19a)

   _____

   (b) How can we praise the Lord in a quiet way, by ourselves? (Verse 19b)

   _____

7. Name two additional forms of praise. (Psalm 47:1a; 134:2a)

   _____

Worship will be as deep and profound as praise is high, exuberant, and powerful.

---

8. What is another way by which we can praise the name of the Lord? (Psalm 149:3a)

   _____

9. List various musical instruments used in biblical times for praising the Lord. (Psalm 150:3b–4; 1 Chronicles 15:16b)

   _____

Part III: Praise God Through Proclamation

10. (a) As we sing to the Lord, what is to be the content of our praises? (Psalm 105:2b)

    _____

(b) In addition to the above, what are we to remember when praising God? Complete the following:

Psalm 105:5b: *"His wonders, and* _____ _____ _____

_____ _____*."*

(c) When we seek the Lord, what should our hearts do? (Verse 3b)

_____

Praise is the declaration of the great and powerful works of God.

---

11. (a) Which of God's *"great wonders"* on behalf of the Israelites are recounted throughout Psalm 136, a psalm of thanksgiving and praise? (Verses 5–25)

_____

_____

_____

_____

_____

_____

(b) To what did the psalmist attribute all this help from God? (Verse 1b and others throughout)

_____

12. (a) To review, what did David say he would meditate on? (Psalm 145:5)

_____

(b) What will God's saints speak of as they bless Him? (Psalm 145:11)

_____

(c) What is the nature of God's kingdom? (Verse 13)

_____

Part IV: Praise God Through Sacrifice

13. (a) What did the writer of Hebrews say we are to continually offer through Jesus Christ? Complete the following:

Hebrews 13:15a: "*Therefore by Him let us continually offer* _____

_____ _____ _____ *to God….*"

(b) How is this praise offered? Complete the following:

Verse 15b: "*…that is,* _____ _____ _____ _____ _____,

_____ _____ *to His name.*"

If we want to live at the forefront of what God is saying and doing,
the sacrifice of praise should become an intrinsic part of our lifestyle.

REFLECTIONS ON THE SACRIFICE OF PRAISE

The Greek word for "*sacrifice*" in Hebrews 13:15 is *thysia*, which actually refers to a victim—a killing. Every sacrifice implies death. In the case of a sacrifice of praise, the victim for the sacrifice is the flesh, or the ego. Praising God always requires a sacrifice because it is something that goes beyond our strength, convenience, desire, and comfort. To praise God, we must kill something ungodly within us, such as apathy, pride, selfishness, worry, fear, bad thoughts, or anything else that keeps us from wholeheartedly expressing His greatness. Our sacrifice releases a movement of the Holy Spirit, who comes to our aid. Then, when the spirit of praise comes, praising ceases to be a sacrifice, as it was in the beginning. By this time, no one has to force us to praise God; our praise becomes spontaneous.

150 The Glory of God

14. What does the Spirit of the Lord give us in exchange for our spirit of heaviness? (Isaiah 61:3a)

_____

15. Summarize, in your own words, the difficult situation Paul and Silas were in when they offered sacrifices of praise. (Acts 16:22b–24 NIV)

_____

_____

16. What happened after they prayed and sang hymns to God? (Acts 16:26 NIV)

_____

_____

17. Significantly, what was the spiritual outcome for the jailer and his family, to whom Paul and Silas proclaimed the gospel? (Acts 16:34b, 33b NIV)

_____

_____

Our priority should be to seek God's glory; then, the signs will follow us.

18. How did Jesus instruct His disciples to respond when they were reviled, persecuted, or falsely accused of evil for the sake of His name? (Matthew 5:12a)

_____

19. In every circumstance of our lives, what manner of glory are we to give to the Lord? (1 Chronicles 16:29a)

_____

Conclusion

When a spiritual atmosphere does not exist for God's presence or glory to manifest, it is a great obstacle to seeing a demonstration of His supernatural power. When I try to minister in such an atmosphere, it is difficult for me to preach the Word because the hearts of the people are not sensitive to receive it. If the spiritual atmosphere is hard, the glory does not descend, and, consequently, few healings and miracles take place.

This is why we must learn to enter into God's presence through both praise and worship, because they work hand in hand. Whether we are worshipping alone or alongside other people, our approach should always be this: praise until the spirit of worship comes, and worship until God's glory descends. This is the key to personal and corporate transformation.

Prayer of Activation

Father of glory, we offer You the sacrifice of praise and the glory due Your name! We remember the marvelous works You have done: Your wonders and the judgments of Your mouth. You are great and greatly to be praised! We praise You in all the circumstances of our lives, and we exalt Your holy name. Pour out Your Spirit in signs and wonders, so that others may believe in Your Son Jesus Christ and receive Your salvation, healing, and deliverance. In Jesus' name, amen.

Action Steps

+ Read the following Scripture verses aloud as you praise God daily, allowing them to instruct you in how to praise Him: Revelation 4:11; Psalm 24:7–10; 105:1–5; 138:1–2. After you finish reading these Scriptures, enter into heartfelt gratitude and thanks for all that God has done for you personally, acknowledging His glorious attributes and ways.

+ Sing praises to the Lord when you undergo any difficult circumstance in your life. Remember the example of Paul and Silas in prison as you sing songs of God's love, power, and grace, and as you release the situation to Him to work in and through.

EXPERIENCES WITH GOD'S GLORY

Healing of a Deaf-Mute Woman

Aneth, a forty-eight-year-old Cuban woman, had been deaf-mute from birth. During a healing and miracle crusade held at King Jesus Ministry, she came forward, claiming her miracle. Pastor Guillermo Maldonado asked the congregation to join together in prayer for her, and he declared her healed. When he laid hands on her, she testified that she felt a "pop" in her ears, and, to the glory of God, she began to hear and speak for the first time in her life! Pastor Maldonado tested her hearing by standing behind her so she could not see him. He began to clap and had her repeat the same beat she had heard. If he clapped once, she clapped once. If he clapped twice, she clapped twice, and so on. It was evident that a miracle had taken place! She was so emotional that she cried, because her dream of hearing and speaking had become a reality.

The saturation of the presence of God, in an atmosphere created by praise and worship, produced the miracle that transformed Aneth's life and the lives of her family members. You can experience the same if you change the way you worship and generate an atmosphere of worship to the true God—an atmosphere where everything is possible!

Study 13

CREATING AN ATMOSPHERE TO BRING HIS PRESENCE, PART 2

"How awesome is this place! This is none other than the house of God, and this is the gate of heaven!"
—Genesis 28:17

Introduction

Worship is more than a declaration; it is a sincere attitude of humility, reverence, respect, and fear of the Lord. In our worship, Jesus must be crowned. He must occupy the throne of our lives—the Holy of Holies within us. We know that faith is a muscle that grows when exercised. Worship works in a similar way; there is always room to go deeper in it. From deep worship will come guidance for the future for an individual, a family, a city, or a nation.

Worship may be expressed by a physical posture, such as bowing the head or body, kneeling, or falling prostrate before the Lord. If we worship in a sincere and humble way, it becomes something that goes well beyond singing or talking to God—it becomes an atmosphere that can be conveyed even through physical contact with others, such as an embrace, through which we transmit everything that flows out of our relationship of worship with the Father.

People who worship in spirit and truth break through to the atmosphere of eternity, where the center of attention is no longer self but God. In His presence, they are not concerned with how they feel or what they are experiencing. They know God requires worship, and this conviction surpasses every temporal situation. Worship is not a feeling but an attitude expressed by one who knows that, without God, he is nothing.

Study Questions

Part I: Honoring the Lord Through Worship

1. In order to honor the Lord properly, we are to worship Him in what way? (1 Chronicles 16:29b)

   _____

2. Who is able to approach the presence of the Lord? (Psalm 24:4a)

   _____

We cannot fake worship or communion with God.

---

3. Recall the type of worshippers the Lord seeks. (John 4:23b)

   _____

<u>KEY DEFINITIONS</u>: Praise focuses on proclaiming the works of God. Worship focuses on the person of God. Praise is initiated by us. Worship is God's answer to our praise. To praise is to seek God. To worship is to be found by Him. Praise increases the anointing. Worship brings the glory. Praise is like building a house for God. Worship is God moving into that house. In praise we talk *about* God. In worship we speak *to* God, and He answers us. In praise we are keenly aware of God's love and greatness. In worship, we are keenly aware of His holiness. Praise is the parade of the King. Worship is His coronation.

---

4. (a) To whom should we *not* give the glory that God is due? (Psalm 115:1a)

   _____

   (b) What two reasons did the psalmist list for giving glory to the name of the Lord? (Verse 1b)

   _____

5. What did the apostle Paul write in his first letter to Timothy as a declaration of worship toward God the King? (1 Timothy 1:17)

    _____

    _____

When a person stops worshipping God, he or she also stops knowing Him.

REFLECTIONS ON WHERE OUR LIFESTYLE OF WORSHIP BEGINS

Each Christian is responsible for "taking" his worship to church with him. In other words, our worship begins at home, in our secret place with Jesus—our prayer closet, office, or car—and it follows us everywhere we go and at all times.

One reason we have not seen God's glory descend upon our lives is that we do not have a continuous and effective private life with Him, which is what allows His presence to be seen in public. Worshipping God in private is an attitude that flows forth, spontaneously and from the heart, when no one sees us, when the responsibility to minister to people is not there, when we do it simply out of love, without seeking any rewards. Those special, private moments cause God to powerfully manifest His presence and to speak and minister directly to our hearts. Our greatest desire should always be to experience new and deeper moments in God's glory because only His presence will transform the human heart. Our efforts cannot accomplish this.

Part II: Revelations of True Worship

6. What language does Scripture use to indicate that true worship is intimate communion with God the Father and Jesus Christ? Complete the following:

    (a) Isaiah 54:5a: "For _____ _____ _____ _____

    _____, the Lord of hosts is His name."

(b) Revelation 21:9b: *"Come, I will show you* _____ _____, _____

_____ _____*."*

(c) What is the Lamb's wife described as having? (Verse 11a)

_____

7. (a) What fundamental aspect of God should we exalt during our worship? (Psalm 34:3a)

_____

(b) Above what is this aspect of God exalted? (Nehemiah 9:5b)

_____

(c) To whom did God give the name that is above every other name? (Philippians 2:9–10a)

_____

(d) What is the proper response to the name of Jesus from all those in heaven and on earth? (Verses 10b–11a)

_____

_____

(e) What will this full acknowledgment of Jesus bring to God the Father? (Verse 11b)

_____

8. There is a recurring phrase in Psalm 119 that serves to remind us not only of the basis on which our intercession should be offered to God, but also our praise and worship. Complete the following as a representative of these phrases:

Psalm 119:25b: *"Revive me* _____ _____ _____

_____*."*

If our worship lacks the Word, God will not honor it or release His power through it.

---

9. Through what means do believers experience God's glory in worship—just as they will when Christ returns, as the below verse indicates? Complete the following:

   Isaiah 40:5a: "*The glory of the* LORD *shall be* _____...."

10. (a) Solomon expressed his heartfelt worship of God at the beginning of his prayer to dedicate the new temple. What did he say as he knelt down and lifted his hands toward heaven? (2 Chronicles 6:14)

    _____

    _____

    _____

    (b) Record how the Lord responded at the end of Solomon's prayer, making His presence known to Solomon and the rest of the Israelites. (2 Chronicles 7:1)

    _____

    _____

11. At the Lord's instruction, the Israelites who were about to enter the Promised Land engaged in worship seven days in a row before they defeated the city of Jericho by God's hand.

    (a) What were Joshua's instructions to the priests for their part in this worship? (Joshua 6:6)

    _____

    (b) Describe the actions of the seven priests carrying the trumpets as they entered into worship. (Verse 8a)

    _____

(c) Where did the armed men march, and where did everyone else march—those who were called the *"rear guard"*? (Joshua 6:9a)

_____

_____

(d) Besides the sound of the trumpets, what other sound was incorporated into the Israelites' worship? (Verse 20a)

_____

(e) When God's people obeyed His instructions for worship, what happened to the wall of Jericho, and what did God's people do? (Verse 20b)

_____

_____

Each time a new sound of worship overflows in a church, the atmosphere changes and old structures are broken.

---

12. When the disciples were gathered *"with one accord"* on the day of Pentecost several weeks after Jesus ascended to heaven, they were likely praying together as they awaited the coming of the Holy Spirit. (See Acts 1:13–14.)

    (a) Describe the sound that could suddenly be heard at the manifestation of God's Spirit. (Acts 2:2a)

    _____

    (b) What other "sounds" were manifest in this visitation by the Spirit? (Verse 4b)

    _____

REFLECTIONS ON "SOUNDS" IN WORSHIP

I have experienced the release of "new sounds" from God through His worshippers in the body of Christ. He is raising up prophetic worshippers who have the ability to interpret and bring down divine sounds from His throne that have a part in fulfilling His plans. The sound that releases God's vision may be the voice of a prophet who proclaims the revelation of His divine determination for the future. When it is difficult for people to understand or believe a revelation from God through words or explanations, then music and prophetic worship can become the means by which they are able to spiritually understand or receive what God is saying and doing.

In light of this reality, we can understand why Satan's attacks within the church are directed mostly at the ministry of praise and worship. Satan is interested in our worship because he knows that God's spiritual power will manifest on earth through it. He knows that if he can stop our worship of God, he can also stop heavenly revelation and sounds from being released on the earth, and thereby hinder God's movement in this generation. We must be alert to his schemes, covering and surrounding the ministry of worship with prayer and intercession.

---

13. (a) As we have learned from previous studies, what should be the result of our experience in God's glory? (2 Corinthians 3:18b)

   _____

   (b) What will happen to those who create and/or trust in idols, something that is the opposite of godly transformation? (Psalm 115:8 NIV)

   _____

The highest level of worship is when we become worship.

Part III: Three Principles for Creating a Spiritual Atmosphere

14. The first principle for creating an atmosphere to bring the presence of God is to "build a spiritual throne" for Him. Let us recall where God is "enthroned," which also applies to His church. (Psalm 22:3b)

   _____

15. The second principle for creating a spiritual atmosphere is that our worship must be of a quality and duration that a "cloud" of His presence is formed.

    (a) Following the example of the psalmist, what should our souls long for as we build a spiritual throne and atmosphere in which God will manifest Himself? (Psalm 84:2a)

    _____

    (b) What should our hearts and flesh cry out for? (Verse 2b)

    _____

16. In previous studies, we have seen that the Lord often speaks from a cloud of His glory. Let us look at another such example.

    (a) When the Israelites in the wilderness were summoned to God's presence, what appeared in the cloud? (Exodus 16:10b)

    _____

    (b) What happened next? (Verse 11a)

    _____

REFLECTIONS ON "BUILDING GOD'S THRONE"

In the spiritual realm, we "build God's throne" when we worship Him. His presence will always manifest when the throne is built. Therefore, we know the throne is complete when we experience the outpouring of His glory. We cannot stop our worship before this happens. Let us always remember this principle: Praise until the spirit of worship comes, and worship until the glory descends. There is no formula for how long we need to praise and worship God; it should always be *until* His spiritual throne is built. The Holy Spirit is our Helper. He teaches us to worship God in spirit and in truth, and He stands by our side to receive our worship and take it to the Father. I firmly believe that our purpose in worship is to invite God's presence to descend. Only in His presence will we be transformed so that we can take the same power of transformation to others.

The ingredients in the atmosphere of glory are continuous prayer,
offerings, intercession, praise, worship, obedience, and honor.

17. The third principle for creating an atmosphere to bring the presence of God is that we must perceive and release the spiritual atmosphere. What did Jacob say when he awoke and remembered his dream of a ladder reaching from earth to heaven, on which God's angels ascended and descended? (Genesis 28:16)

    _____

18. Who alone will enable us to perceive a spiritual atmosphere in which God is present? Complete the following:

    1 Corinthians 2:12: *"Now we have received, not the spirit of the world, but* _____

    _____ _____ ____ _____ _____*, that we*

    might know the things that have been freely given to us by God."

19. What do we need to "mix" with a spiritual atmosphere of worship in order to release and receive God's blessings? This is the ingredient that the Israelites in the wilderness failed to mix with the word they heard from God. (Hebrews 4:2b)

    _____

A spiritual atmosphere is created through worship,
but the cloud must be discerned to release its contents.

Part IV: Responding to God's Glory

20. (a) Immediately after having the dream of a ladder reaching to heaven and God speaking to him, what did Jacob say about the place where he was? (Genesis 28:17)

    _____

    _____

    (b) The morning after he had his dream, in what way did Jacob respond to the fact that the Lord was *"in this place"* with him? (Verse 18)

    _____

    _____

21. When Moses first found himself in the presence of God, what did the Lord instruct him to do after cautioning him not to draw near to the burning bush, and what reason did He give? (Exodus 3:5b)

_____

_____

22. Recall the prophet Isaiah's vision of the Lord in His glory. (See Isaiah 6:1–4.)

(a) What did Isaiah say when he found himself before God's throne? (Verse 5)

_____

_____

(b) Once Isaiah was assured that he had received forgiveness for his sin, enabling him to stand in God's presence, what was the first thing he said after hearing God ask, "*Who will go for Us?*" (Verse 8b)

_____

23. What did Jeremiah ask the Lord to do for him as his "*praise*"? (Jeremiah 17:14a)

_____

24. (a) When Jesus was teaching at a certain house, what was present in the spiritual atmosphere there to heal the people—including various Pharisees and teachers of the law—who had gathered to hear Him? (Luke 5:17b)

_____

(b) Does the text indicate that any of the Pharisees, teachers of the law, or others present were healed? (Verse 17)

_____

(c) A paralyzed man on a bed was then lowered into the house through an opening in the roof by some men who had carried him there. What do the Scriptures give as the reason why this paralyzed man was forgiven and healed that day? (Luke 5:20a)

_____

(d) How did the onlookers respond to this healing? (Verse 26)

_____

Conclusion

We need to have continuous experiences with God's presence in order to be transformed into the image of Christ and to manifest His power. To have these experiences, we must discern that He is indeed present with us in His glory. Is it possible for us to be in the same place where the glory of God is present and not realize it? Yes, it is possible. Remember that it happened to Jacob. There are many reasons why this may happen, but, most often, it is because of our sins, such as bitterness, resentment, and a lack of forgiveness. Another reason is that we can become totally absorbed in our own problems, so that our spiritual perception is dulled or even completely turned off. We need to remain sensitive to how the Spirit of God is moving. That way, the next time we recognize His presence, we can respond in faith and worship.

In the presence of God, there is salvation, healing, deliverance, transformation, visions, dreams, prophecy, revelation, impartation, and activation. Let me define the last two terms. In the glory, God shares (or transmits) portions of His virtue, anointing, power, favor, grace, gifts, and so forth, with us. Whatever we receive from Him is an *impartation*. An impartation is something that we did not previously have; it was added to us. (See Romans 1:11.) For instance, after you have been in the glory, you may find that people are often healed when you pray for them, when formerly this was not the case. *Activation* occurs when God "awakens" or "stirs up" gifts that He has already given to us but that lay buried within us—due to our fear, lack of knowledge, apathy, or another obstacle. (See 2 Timothy 1:6.) God may activate a dormant gift within anyone who enters His presence.

In the glory, we can hear God's voice and become fired up to go and give to others what we have received. God's purpose for manifesting His glory is to enable us to take it to a lost world—to people without God, faith, or hope. Our experiences in His presence must be carried to our workplaces, schools, and community organizations; they must be taken wherever we go: restaurants, department stores, supermarkets, and the streets. They must be shared with our entire circle of influence. God's glory will give us the boldness we need to preach His

Word, speak of Jesus, heal the sick, deliver the captives, and do miracles. Let us make the decision right now to take His glory to everyone around us, even to all the nations of the earth!

Prayer of Activation

Father of glory, You are the King eternal, immortal, and invisible! You alone are wise. Let honor and glory be Yours forever. We want to praise You until the spirit of worship comes and worship You until Your glory descends. Open our eyes to recognize Your presence and Your glory as we respond to You in spirit and in truth. Then, impart to us Your salvation, healing, deliverance, revelation, transformation, and activation for service. In Jesus' name, amen!

Action Steps

+ Psalm 24:4 says that *"he who has clean hands and a pure heart"* may stand in God's presence. Before praising and worshipping God, confess your sins to Him and receive His forgiveness and cleansing.

+ Spend a good portion of your devotional time with God in worship. Begin by expressing gratitude for His faithfulness and for what He's done in your life. Worship Him as your Lord and King, mentioning His attributes. Talk to Him as your heavenly Father, declaring your love for Him and telling Him of your willingness to obey whatever He tells you to do. Ask Him to enable you to discern the spiritual atmosphere of His presence, as He reaches out to you in healing, deliverance, and revelation for your life. Then, wait on Him, listening to hear what He wants to speak to you at that moment.

EXPERIENCES WITH GOD'S GLORY

A Boy Healed of Spina Bifida

At a miracle and healing service in Argentina in which Pastor Guillermo Maldonado ministered, glorious testimonies were heard from among the twenty-two thousand people who had gathered. A couple came forward with their three-year-old son, Jeremiah, who was born with spina bifida. This condition had affected the boy's muscles, causing his legs to be twisted. He was unable to place his feet on the floor or to stand on his own, even if he was held by the hands. Not only that, but his condition had caused hydrocephalus (increased fluid around the brain) and the need for diapers because he had no bladder control. To get him to the healing service, his parents had to travel two thousand kilometers (more than 1,200 miles), believing the Lord would do a miracle.

During the worship, the child began to be healed. When his parents realized what was taking place, they ran from the back of the stadium, where they were seated, to the platform. With the help of doctors and pastors, they began to test Jeremiah. The parents removed the equipment the doctors had placed on his legs to straighten them out, and he began to take his first steps, just like any child who is first learning to walk. When they saw that he was able to plant his feet on the floor, they knew his legs were straight. A doctor explained that this was a creative miracle because the fact that Jeremiah was able to stand on his own and straighten up to walk was a sign that his nerves had recovered life and movement. God corrected the defects in his spine and nerves, restoring the normal functioning of his lower limbs and bladder. Jeremiah's parents were deeply moved to see their son healed before their eyes! They cried and thanked God because they had waited for so long for a miracle. They had come from so far away, believing that God would hear their cry, and they were not disappointed. It all took place in His manifest presence. When we are full of God's presence, the creative miracles manifest everywhere; there is nothing His glory cannot do.

Ignited by the Fire of God

"He will baptize you with the Holy Spirit and fire."
—Matthew 3:11

Introduction

God's glory has many facets, and only He, in His absolute sovereignty, can decide which aspect He will manifest—and when. One aspect of His glory is *"a consuming fire"* (see, for example, Deuteronomy 4:24; Hebrews 12:29), which can descend to bring judgment on earth. But because God's glory burns everything that is not holy, His fire also purifies and sanctifies His people who have turned from their wicked ways and who yearn to live in righteousness and justice, filled with the Holy Spirit.

In the world today, spiritual darkness is becoming thicker and opposition to the spirit of Christ stronger; challenges are intensifying, and believers have to be ready to meet these circumstances. We must walk in the fire of God's presence so that we will know how to alleviate human suffering and bring people to Christ in the midst of these momentous last days.

God's fire is not for those who do not desire to live holy and pure lives. The people of Israel were afraid of this fire, and the root of that fear was their unwillingness to pay the price demanded by it. This attitude can be seen today among believers in the church of Christ. Many people reject God's revivals, power, glory, and miracles because they are afraid of His presence and because they do not want to pay the price required to keep His fire burning.

In this study, we will explore what is meant by the fact that God is an all-consuming fire. Furthermore, we will learn what it means for us to be full of the Holy Spirit and His fire. We will come to understand the purpose for the fire of His presence, what it produces in us, and how to keep it burning. This will encourage us to go and gather the great and final harvest of souls prepared by the Lord before His coming.

Study Questions

Part I: The Fire of God

1. In the previous chapter, we learned that the Lord taught Moses to revere His presence by telling him to take off his sandals in recognition of the holy ground on which he was standing.

    (a) In what form did Moses initially encounter the manifestation of God's presence through the *"Angel of the LORD"*? (Exodus 3:2)

    _____

    _____

    (b) From where did the Lord speak to Moses? (Verse 4b)

    _____

> *When Moses had the experience with the burning bush,*
> *he received the fire of God's presence.*

---

2. What continual reminder of the fire of God was with the nation of Israel? (Exodus 13:21b)

    _____

3. In what manner did the glory of the Lord appear to the Israelites at the top of Mount Sinai? (Exodus 24:17)

    _____

4. What did Moses tell the Israelites after urging them to heed the covenant the Lord had made with them and not to turn to idolatry? (Deuteronomy 4:24)

    _____

5. In the book of Isaiah, the Lord's holiness and justice are described as *"devouring fire"* and *"everlasting burnings."* (See Isaiah 30:27, 30; 33:14.) What did Isaiah say about who is able to dwell with this type of fire? Complete the following:

Isaiah 33:15a: *"He who* _____ _____

_____ _____ _____.*"*

6. What are we taught by the grace of God that brings salvation? (Titus 2:12)

_____

_____

_____

Many people want to be holy but do not want to pay the price of being sanctified.

---

7. (a) What is a major aspect of God's will for us? Complete the following:

1 Thessalonians 4:3: *"For this is the will of God, your* _____.*"*

(b) What did Paul pray that the God of peace would do in a complete way for the Thessalonians? (1 Thessalonians 5:23a)

_____

(c) List the three aspects of the human makeup, which Paul desired would be preserved blameless in the Thessalonians at the coming of the Lord Jesus Christ. (Verse 23b)

_____

(d) Who would accomplish this preservation, and why? (Verse 24)

_____

8. Who is our Advocate with the Father when we sin and fail to live in righteousness and holiness? (1 John 2:1b)

_____

Part II: Jesus Came to Bring Power and Fire

9. In what two ways did John say that Jesus would baptize us? (Matthew 3:11b)

_____

KEY DEFINITION: The Greek word for *"baptize"* in Matthew 3:11 is *baptizo*, which means "to dip" and "to make fully wet." This word was used to describe the event of a boat being covered or submerged by a great wave, and this is essentially what happens when we are baptized in water by immersion. We are completely covered, totally submerged underwater. The same experience occurs when we are baptized with the Holy Spirit and fire. We are submerged in the consuming fire of the presence of God so that it affects our whole being.

10. What did Jesus say He had come to send on the earth? (Luke 12:49)

_____

11. What did Jesus tell His disciples they would be endued with when *"the Promise,"* the Holy Spirit, came upon them? (Luke 24:49b; Acts 1:8a)

_____

You cannot impart the fire until you have a burning-bush experience.

12. What would be the result of this enduement? (Acts 1:8b)

_____

KEY DEFINITION: The Greek word translated *"power"* in Luke 24:49 and Acts 1:8 is *dunamis*, meaning "force" or "miraculous power." This is the word from which we derive the terms *dynamic* and *dynamite*, with the implication of "explosive power."

13. This enduement of power was noticeable in the disciples as they preached the good news of the kingdom and performed healings and miracles in Jesus' name. What did some people in Thessalonica who opposed the disciples say about them? (Acts 17:6b)

_____

14. What does the Holy Spirit do in the world through our witness and the miraculous works we perform in His power? (John 16:8)

_____

*The individual with an experience of God's power
is no longer at the mercy of anyone's opinion.*

REFLECTIONS ON THE TRANSFORMING NATURE OF GOD'S FIRE

The burning bush that Moses saw was not consumed because the fire of God never burns out. This manifestation pointed to the eternity of the Lord and to the passion for God that would burn in the heart of Moses. Moses' heart had been transformed forever in his experience with the burning bush. God released in him the same passion He had to deliver the people of Israel, who were being held captive in Egypt. One moment in the fire of God led Moses to deliver a people whom he had not delivered in the course of his eighty years, even though he had tried to do so in his own strength as a young man. Moses became a faithful friend of God, a leader of millions, a man zealous to do the will of his Lord—performing miracles, signs, and wonders by God's hand and speaking with Him face-to-face. None of this would have taken place, or would have been even remotely imaginable, without the burning-bush experience. It was only after this encounter that he was able to believe, rise up, and lead an entire nation to receive its inheritance in the Promised Land. This change was caused by the fire of the presence of God!

You can have a similar experience. God is the living God who continues to do miracles among His people. He has a special mission for you to carry out—the reason why you were created—and He will give you His fire to empower you to see it through, a fire that will never burn out. Whatever you have been unable to do up until now, you will do with the fire of God.

Part III: Ten Purposes of the Fire of God

15. One purpose of the fire of God is to generate a passion for saving souls.

    (a) How did Jesus describe His followers? (Matthew 5:14a)

    _____

    (b) For what purpose must we allow the light of God's glory to shine through us to the world? (Verse 16)

    _____

We cannot be light if we are not on fire.

---

16. A second purpose of God's fire is to bring judgment. In the Bible, we see that God sometimes sent His holy fire for the purpose of judging those who blatantly disregarded Him and His commands.

    (a) What happened to the cities of Sodom and Gomorrah due to their multiple transgressions and profound iniquity? (Genesis 19:24)

    _____

    (b) What happened to the sons of Aaron, who were God's priests, when they offered *"profane fire"* before the Lord? (Leviticus 10:2)

    _____

    (c) What are now being reserved for fire until the final day of judgment? (2 Peter 3:7a)

    _____

Each time the earth fills with corruption and violence,
God brings His judgment to purify it—usually through fire.

---

17. A third purpose of the fire of God is to purify and sanctify His people.

    (a) How is the Lord's judgment of believers different from His judgment against the world? (1 Corinthians 11:32)

    _____

    _____

    (b) What should we be doing so that the Lord has no need to chasten us? (Verse 31)

    _____

    (c) What should we ask God to do for us as we undertake the above process, and why? (Psalm 139:23–24)

    _____

    _____

God's fire falls only where there is sacrifice
because it proves that what was offered to God is real.

---

18. A fourth purpose of God's fire is to reveal our true motives and the genuineness of our faith.

    (a) To what is the Messiah compared? (Malachi 3:2b)

    _____

    (b) In what manner will He *"sit"*? (Verse 3a)

    _____

    (c) For what purpose will He refine His people? (Verse 3b)

    _____

19. In what way did Peter describe the testing of our faith through various trials and persecutions? Complete the following:

    1 Peter 1:7: *"…that the genuineness of your faith, being much more precious than gold that perishes, though _____ _____ _____ _____ _____, may be found to praise, honor, and glory at the revelation of Jesus Christ."*

20. On the day of judgment, what will the fire of God test? (1 Corinthians 3:13b)

    _____

21. A fifth purpose of God's fire is to produce within us a passion to fulfill our callings.

    (a) In what way did the prophet Jeremiah describe the word that God had put in his heart, which he tried to suppress? Complete the following:

    Jeremiah 20:9b: *"But His word was in my heart _____ _____*

    _____ _____ _____ _____ _____ _____

    _____…."

    (b) Was Jeremiah successful in holding back what God had placed within him to tell the Israelites? (Verse 9b)

    _____

The fire of the presence of God releases the passion that is in Him.

REFLECTIONS ON REKINDLING ONE'S GIFTS

In 2 Timothy 1:6, the apostle Paul urged Timothy to stir up the fire of the gift of the Holy Spirit he had imparted to him, that Timothy had already received, and that had been active in the beginning. The Greek word translated *"stir up"* is *anazopureo*, which means "to rekindle." First, we must stir up our personal gifts so that, later, with the same fire, we can help others to stir up their gifts. This demands a decision on our part to seek to be ignited by God's fire.

22. A sixth purpose for the fire of God is to produce within us a passion to persevere and to overcome opposition to God and the gospel.

    (a) What did Jesus endure during His challenging ministry, His unjust trials and interrogations by religious and political leaders, and His agonizing death on the cross, because of His passion for God and *"the joy that was set before Him"* (Hebrews 12:2)? (Verse 3a)

    _____

    (b) List various difficulties and trials the apostle Paul endured for the sake of the gospel, with an endurance initially fueled by the fire of his encounter with Jesus on the road to Damascus. (2 Corinthians 11:23b–28 NIV)

    _____

    _____

    _____

    _____

    _____

    _____

Discipline earns the admiration of others, but passion is contagious.

---

23. A seventh purpose of God's fire is to produce a passion within us to know Him intimately.

    (a) Recall the reasons why Paul said he counted as loss everything that previously had been gain to him. (Philippians 3:8)

    _____

    _____

(b) What were among Paul's highest spiritual goals? (Philippians 3:10)

_____

_____

> **When the old atmosphere is changed by an atmosphere of glory,**
> **then hunger and thirst for God are produced in people's spirits.**

---

24. An eighth purpose of the fire of God is to produce supernatural boldness in us.

    (a) What did the religious leaders see and perceive about Peter and John that caused them to marvel? (Acts 4:13a)

    _____

    (b) What did these leaders realize? (Verse 13b)

    _____

25. After Peter and John were warned by the religious leaders not to speak or teach in the name of Jesus, they met with their companions and prayed to the Lord.

    (a) What is one thing they asked for? (Acts 4:29b)

    _____

    (b) What happened to them as a result of this prayer? (Verse 31b)

    _____

    _____

REFLECTIONS ON BAPTISM WITH FIRE

There are believers who have received the infilling of the Holy Spirit with the evidence of speaking in other tongues and who have been filled with power from heaven, yet they never testify of Jesus. Neither do they pray for the sick or cast out demons. They have the dynamite, but it has not been lighted with fire.

When the fire no longer burns, regardless of how much oil there is, the lampstand will not shine. Likewise, we cannot be powerful, effective witnesses of Jesus if our lamps have not been lit with the fire of the glory of God. Christians who are passive and indifferent have either lost the fire or never received it to begin with.

Baptism with fire takes place when we go before God so that He can set us ablaze with the same kind of passion that burns in His heart—the passion to be witnesses of Jesus and to bring the truth of the dominion, lordship, and will of the King to earth by doing miracles in His name and by His hand.

---

26. A ninth purpose of God's fire is to produce a passion to see miracles, signs, and wonders as a confirmation of the gospel message.

    (a) What did Peter and John and their companions ask the Lord to do in connection with their prayer for boldness? (Acts 4:30)

    _____

    _____

    (b) In what way was this prayer answered? (Acts 5:12a)

    _____

27. A tenth purpose of the fire of God is to produce revival. Jesus' anointing was one that brought physical, emotional, mental, social, and spiritual transformation to people's lives, and it is an anointing He has passed on to us through the indwelling Holy Spirit. For a review, record the various aspects of this anointing. (Luke 4:18–19)

    _____

    _____

    _____

Jesus comes for a church that is not only experiencing revival
but also is on fire for the harvest.

Conclusion

While Jesus ministered on earth, His greatest passion was to release the fire of God's presence so that, after His resurrection, multitudes of people around the world could reproduce His miracles and lead men and women to know the Father with the same passion that He had. In addition to providing for our salvation, this is the reason He went to the cross and died. When He was resurrected, a baptism of fire was released over the disciples at Pentecost, and they immediately began to shake up the world.

Every believer needs to have such an experience. It helps us to produce supernatural evidence proving that Jesus indeed lives. Without it, we will have only an *opinion* about supernatural power—pure theory. However, once we experience the fire, we will ignite in a never-ending passion that will lead to the demonstration of supernatural power. We will also be able to transfer that power to others, in order to release revivals, healings, miracles, signs, and wonders. These manifestations will deliver individual people, cities, and nations from the bondage of sin, sickness, and curses.

Prayer of Activation

Father of glory, thank You for all the students who are learning about Your glory through this Bible study. May those who have never before been filled with power through the baptism of the Holy Spirit with the evidence of speaking in other tongues be filled right now. Release the fire of Your presence to everyone who hungers for it. Submerge and ignite them in it. May they be filled with Your power and fire! We have absolute faith that Your fire is burning within us right now. In the name of Jesus, amen!

Action Steps

+ Whenever you seem to lose your fire and passion for God, ask the Holy Spirit to release that fire and passion within you once again. Use Psalm 139:23–24 as your prayer, and ask the Lord to search your heart for any wrong attitudes so that you can repent and return to Him.

+ When you experience the fire of God's presence, do not be afraid, knowing that it is for your sanctification, not your condemnation. Respond in submission, humility, faith, and obedience.

+ Once the fire of God is ignited in you, go as an instrument of the Lord and be a witness of Jesus. Tell others about the gospel of salvation in Jesus, pray for and lay hands on the sick for healing, and cast out demons. Seek to use the various spiritual gifts and abilities that God has given you, as the Spirit works through you.

EXPERIENCES WITH GOD'S GLORY

A Life Rescued and a Ministry of Fire on the Streets of Miami

Andy is a young man who grew up in a dysfunctional family. His father hadn't met his own father until the age of eighteen, and his grandfather had lost his father at the age of two. A generational curse of broken homes, divorce, and adultery was afflicting the lives of this young man and his family members. Andy's father was physically and verbally violent; this caused Andy to feel strong hated and rejection toward him. Later, this hatred turned into rebelliousness. As a teenager, he entered the world of drugs and gangs, where he met people who felt the same way he did. Instead of finding answers to his pain, he found a faster way to deepen the depression, sense of lost identity, and lack of paternal love he felt inside. Life meant nothing to him. Finally, he decided to commit suicide.

Yet, on the night he had chosen to take his life, he heard a voice say, "Don't do it. I have a purpose for you." The voice brought such deep conviction to his heart that he fell to his knees and began to cry—after years of not being able to shed a single tear due to his hardened heart. That night, he asked God to enter his heart and change his life. He had never felt a love so true and so pure as the love of the heavenly Father, and he was never the same again. Andy completely fell in love with God. He left behind the drugs, illicit sex, gangs, delinquency, and unforgiveness. In place of these things, he began to attend the early-morning prayer sessions at King Jesus Ministry and was trained in prayer.

Andy became a youth pastor of the church, and, today, he faithfully serves God. He is producing a spiritual revolution among the youth, activating them in the gifts of words of knowledge, prophecy, and deliverance to evangelize the streets of Miami with signs, wonders, and tremendous fruit. He has multiplied himself in others who are also on fire for Christ—young people who provide pastoral care and who witness as he does, under the slogan "Street Glory." This group goes out every Saturday to evangelize the streets, invading the entire city—including the dangerous zones. In the first fifteen weeks of Street Glory, these young people harvested over six thousand professions of faith. Street Glory is now expanding into Washington, D.C., New York, Mexico, Venezuela, Argentina, Guatemala, Spain, and England. At twenty-six years old, Andy imparts the fire of heaven to youth leaders who are under the spiritual covering of King Jesus Ministry. God is raising up the fire generation!

Study 15

EARTHEN VESSELS CHOSEN TO CARRY HIS GLORY

"But we have this treasure in earthen vessels,
that the excellence of the power may be of God and not of us."
—2 Corinthians 4:7

Introduction

From the beginning of creation, God intended men and women to live and walk in His glory—to be carriers of His presence. As we have seen, His purpose has always been to dwell in us. That is why He deposited in us His breath of life and why He regards us as the supreme beings among His creation, crowned with glory and honor. (See Psalm 8:5.)

Human beings were the first tabernacle of the presence of God. Yet, from the moment man sinned and fell away from God's glory, God no longer had a physical dwelling place in which to reside. Then came the unfolding of His plan of restoration. He made Jesus—who was fully human as well as fully God—a dwelling place, a home, a tabernacle for Himself. Jesus walked on earth as *"Immanuel,"* which means *"God with us"* (Matthew 1:23). God the Father dwelled in His Son, who came to heal the sick and deliver those who were oppressed by the devil. Then, after Jesus paid the price for humanity's sin on the cross and rose again, the spirits of humans were made new to receive the gift of God's Holy Spirit within them. And it is God's plan that we "carry" His glory wherever we go.

Study Questions

Part I: The Former Glory

1. What did the Lord declare through the prophet Haggai about the manifestation of His glory on earth? (Haggai 2:9a)

---

2. Under what period was the former glory? Complete the following:

Luke 16:16a: "_____ _____ _____ _____

_____ *were until John* [the Baptist]."

3. Briefly summarize some of the supernatural acts that took place during the former glory, several of which we looked at in previous studies:

(a) Exodus 14:21–22, 29:

_____

(b) Exodus 13:21:

_____

(c) Exodus 15:23–25:

_____

(d) Joshua 6:20:

_____

(e) 1 Kings 17:9–16:

_____

_____

(f) 2 Kings 5:1–14:

_____

(g) 2 Kings 13:20–21:

_____

(h) Daniel 3:13–27:

_____

Part II: A New Dwelling Place for God's Glory

4. When the Word (Jesus) *"became flesh and dwelt among us"* (John 1:14a), what did His disciples witness in Him? Complete the following:

Verse 14b: *"…and we beheld* _____ _____, _____

_____ _____ _____ _____ _____

_____ _____ _____ _____,

full of grace and truth."

5. Jesus' life and ministry, including the healings and miracles He performed, bridged the former glory and the latter glory, but He lived under the law until His resurrection. What reason did Jesus give John to explain why He needed to be baptized by him? (Matthew 3:15b)

_____

6. What did Jesus say He came to do in relation to the Law and the Prophets? (Matthew 5:17b) Choose one of the following by circling the letter:

   (a) fulfill them

   (b) destroy them

   (c) reject them

   (d) ignore them

7. The incarnation of God in Jesus Christ marked the first time since the fall of humanity that God had dwelled in a Man. Recall what Jesus declared when He prayed to the Father regarding those who had believed—and would believe—in Him. (John 17:22)

_____

8. On what day did the latter glory fully arrive on earth with the outpouring of the Holy Spirit? (Acts 2:1a)

_____

We are carriers of God's presence through His indwelling Spirit.

Part III: The Latter Glory

9. The glory of the *"latter temple"* (Haggai 2:9) is greater than the former because of what Jesus accomplished through His death and resurrection.

   (a) What did Paul say a believer's physical body is? (1 Corinthians 6:19a)

   _____

   (b) What Old Testament prophecy did Paul quote when emphasizing that the church as a whole is also *"the temple of the living God"*? (2 Corinthians 6:16b)

   _____

   _____

10. What did Paul say all the members of the body of Christ—together—grow into? Complete the following:

   Ephesians 2:21–22: *"…in whom the whole building, being fitted together, grows*

   into _____ _____ _____ _____ _____

   _____, *in whom you also are being built together for* _____

   _____ _____ ____ _____ *in the Spirit."*

11. (a) What do believers have as an inheritance through Jesus under the latter glory? (Ephesians 1:18b)

   _____

(b) In Paul's metaphor, where do we currently have these riches, or *"treasure"*? (2 Corinthians 4:7a)

_____

(c) What is the reason for this? (Verse 7b)

_____

12. (a) What did Paul call the vessels on whom God has bestowed *"the riches of His glory"*? (Romans 9:23a)

_____

(b) For what had God prepared these vessels beforehand? (Verse 23b)

_____

13. The following Scripture explains further why the latter glory, which comes from the ministry of Jesus, is *"more excellent"* than the former glory. Complete the following:

Hebrews 8:6: *"He [Jesus] is also Mediator of* _____ _____

_____, *which was established on* _____

_____.*"*

14. What did Jesus say believers would do under the latter glory, because He was going to the Father? (John 14:12b)

_____

Part IV: Demonstrating God's Glory on Earth

15. The first several verses of Isaiah 60 illustrate the glory of God that is within us and upon us, as well as how we demonstrate that glory to the world.

What is the first word in Isaiah 60:1, which tells us how we begin to manifest God's glory?

_____

16. (a) What quotation did Paul include in his letter to the Ephesians that combined the idea of light from Isaiah 60:1 and the concept of resurrection/new life from Isaiah 26:19? (Ephesians 5:14)

_____

(b) There are two action words in this quotation, which are spiritual calls to action. One is "*arise.*" What is the other? (Verse 14)

_____

We cannot see the manifest presence of God if we are not seeking it.

---

17. (a) What is the second word in Isaiah 60:1, which encourages us to reflect God's glory?

_____

(b) How did Paul depict the influence of the Philippian believers who, "*in the midst of a crooked and perverse generation*" (Philippians 2:15a), were "*holding fast the word of life*" (verse 16a)? Complete the following:

Verse 15b: "*…among whom* _____ _____ _____

_____ _____ _____ _____.*"*

KEY DEFINITION: The word "*shine*" in Isaiah 60:1 is translated from the Hebrew word *owr*, whose definitions include "to be or become light," "to be luminous," "to give, show light," and even "to set on fire."

---

18. The third aspect of Isaiah 60:1, which illustrates God's manifest glory, is the phrase "*for your light has come.*"

(a) What did the apostle John say about the life that was in Jesus? (John 1:4b)

_____

(b) When Christ's brilliant light shone on Saul (Paul) on the road to Damascus, and Saul fell to the ground, what was one of the first things Christ said to him, reminiscent of the statement *"Arise"* in Isaiah 60:1? Complete the following:

Acts 26:16a: *"But* _____ _____ _____ _____

_____ _____."

(c) After Paul had experienced and received Christ's light, what was he sent to do for those who did not know Christ—a calling that we share today? Complete the following:

Verse 18a: *"To open their eyes, in order* _____ _____ _____

_____ _____ _____ _____, _____

_____ _____ _____ _____ _____

_____ _____....*"

(d) When we fulfill this calling, what do we enable people to receive? (Verse 18b)

_____

_____

Darkness is the terrifying influence of Satan's kingdom on earth. Light is the glory of God that removes the darkness.

REFLECTIONS ON THE FORMER AND LATTER GLORY

I believe the latter glory is effectively the union of the former glory and the latter glory; it magnifies the power that is released and the wonders of which we testify. The manifestations of this new glory are taking place in the present, and we will see them in their fullness in the future. Through Christ, we can live within the dimensions of faith and glory, having the ability to experience the manifestations of God's glory in the *now*—all because Jesus conquered the cross and was raised from the dead!

What manifestations can we expect to see in the latter glory? We can expect to see an acceleration of God's work in every area, as well as radical transformations; miracles, signs, and wonders; the casting out of demons; millions of souls won for Christ; dominion over nature; supernatural provision and protection; the shaking of cities, nations, and continents by revivals produced by the glory of God; and other phenomena we cannot fathom.

---

19. (a) How did Isaiah describe the glory of the Lord coming upon His people, using imagery related to the natural sun? (Isaiah 60:1b)

_____

(b) When the father of John the Baptist prophesied of the coming Messiah, what similar words did he use? Complete the following:

Luke 1:78b (NIV): "*...because of the tender mercy of our God, by which* _____

_____ _____ _____ _____ _____

_____ _____ _____."

(c) What would the Messiah do when He came? (Verse 79a NIV)

_____

(d) What examples of miracles and signs did Jesus give John the Baptist as proof that He was the "*rising sun*" of whom his father had prophesied? (Matthew 11:5)

_____

_____

_____

KEY DEFINITION: The *Amplified Bible* provides insight into the meanings of the words "*Arise*" and "*Shine*" in Isaiah 60:1: "*Arise [from the depression and prostration in which circumstances have kept you—rise to a new life]! Shine (be radiant with the glory of the Lord), for your light has come, and the glory of the Lord has risen upon you!"*

20. When God's glory rises upon us, and we receive it, then *"His glory will be seen upon [us]"* (Isaiah 60:2b).

    (a) In what manner was God's glory literally seen upon Stephen by the religious council when he came before them after being falsely charged with blasphemy? (Acts 6:15b)

    _____

    (b) How was God's glory "seen" upon Paul in a special way? (Acts 19:11–12)

    _____

    _____

21. (a) What did Isaiah say will happen on the earth in the days of the latter glory, even as God's glory is upon His people? (Isaiah 60:2a)

    _____

    (b) What are some of the forms that this dire situation has taken and will take before Christ's return? (Matthew 24:6a, 7, 9–12; Luke 21:11b)

    _____

    _____

    _____

    (c) What is the "good news" in this scenario? (Matthew 24:14)

    _____

    _____

(d) What did Paul exhort believers to do in relation to *"unfruitful works of darkness"*? (Ephesians 5:11a)

_____

(e) Because they were *"once darkness"* but now are *"light in the Lord"* (Ephesians 5:8), in what manner are believers to walk as children of light, bearing the fruit of the Spirit? Complete the following:

Verse 9: *"For the fruit of the Spirit is in* _____ _____,

_____, _____ _____."

(f) What did Paul urge believers to do as they walk in the light of Christ circumspectly and wisely, and for what reason? (Verse 16)

_____

The glory of God can manifest in any of His aspects—visible and invisible—here and now.

---

22. (a) Whom did Isaiah say would come to God's people when they saw the glory that was upon them? (Isaiah 60:3)

_____

(b) In an Old Testament example of this concept, whom did Pharaoh call upon when he needed a supernatural explanation for his unusual dream, which turned out to be a prophetic word about his nation's future? (Genesis 41:14–15)

_____

(c) Whom did this person clarify would interpret the dream for Pharaoh? (Verse 16)

_____

(d) Who was one of the first Gentile officials to be converted to Christ by the gospel? (Acts 10)

_____

(e) What did Jesus tell His disciples was the reason they would be brought before rulers and kings for His sake? (Mark 13:9b)

_____

23. (a) What did Isaiah say about the *"sons"* and *"daughters"* of those on whom the glory of the Lord had risen? (Isaiah 60:4b)

_____

(b) What did God say He would do for the descendants and offspring of His people? (Isaiah 44:3b)

_____

(c) What else would the children of God's people experience from the Lord, and what would they have? (Isaiah 54:13)

_____

24. (a) What did Isaiah say would come to those on whom God's light had shone? Complete the following:

Isaiah 60:5b: "…_____ _____ _____ _____

_____ *shall come to you.*"

(b) Just before the Lord freed the Israelites from slavery in Egypt, what did He tell His people to do? (Exodus 11:2; 12:35)

_____

(c) What had the Lord given to His people in the sight of the Egyptians, and what did the Egyptians grant them? (Exodus 12:36)

_____

(d) What did Solomon say is stored up for the righteous? (Proverbs 13:22b)

_____

25. What did the Lord say He would do in blessing His people and drawing the Gentiles to His light? Complete the following:

Isaiah 60:7b: "*And I will* _____ _____ _____ _____

_____ _____."

Conclusion

Every member of the body of Christ is responsible for carrying, protecting, and manifesting God's glory on earth. We are the temple built not by men but by God's hand, where His presence dwells by the Holy Spirit.

The glory of God can still come *upon* us, the same as it did upon various servants of God in the Old Testament, as well as the early Christians. (See, for example, Acts 11:15; 19:6.) However, God's glory is also *within* us, just as it was for those early Christians who believed in Jesus and received the indwelling Holy Spirit. This is what it means for the former and the latter glory to be active together!

Carnal or worldly individuals do not understand that God is supernatural; they feel there is no purpose for the spiritual realm because they are in darkness and cannot see it. It is our responsibility and task to demonstrate it—to show them the light of Christ and miracles done in His name. No one can "explain" God, but when people experience Him, no explanations are needed. If we find ourselves trying to give explanations, it is because religion has separated us from experience. People will believe God when they experience Him. When they see the supernatural things that take place through us, they will realize that this remarkable power comes from God alone. At this realization, they will begin to glorify Him. It is wonderful to know that, wherever we go, this "*treasure*" (2 Corinthians 4:7) that dwells in us has the ability to save, heal, deliver, and transform. The only requisite is that we make ourselves available to manifest His glory.

Prayer of Activation

Father of glory, we are earthen vessels, ready to carry Your glory to those around us. May Your glory rise upon us now, so that we may awaken, arise, and shine as reflections of Your grace, power, and majesty to the world. Bring multitudes to faith in Jesus, and pour out Your healing and miracles in the "*greater works*" Jesus promised. Glorify the house of Your glory, now and for eternity. Amen!

Action Steps

+ Your body is the *"temple of the Holy Spirit"* (1 Corinthians 6:19). Consider if there is any way in which you are mistreating this *"temple"*—through overeating, substance abuse, neglect of exercise, and so forth—and stop doing it. Determine to honor the Lord with your entire life, including your physical body.

+ We must learn to walk circumspectly and wisely in these last days, and to redeem the time, *"because the days are evil"* (Ephesians 5:16). Write down what you can do this week and this month to redeem your time to better fulfill God's purposes of manifesting His glory to the world. Each week, review what you have written and renew your commitment to redeeming your time.

EXPERIENCES WITH GOD'S GLORY

Raised from the Dead to Minister God's Resurrection Power

In Lima, Peru, Pastor César Augusto Atoche was rushed to the hospital due to an obstruction in his coronary artery. He underwent a double bypass. Immediately after the surgery, he suffered a fatal heart attack. The doctors did all that was humanly possible to resuscitate him, but to no avail. They left the operating room disheartened and informed his wife that he had died. Pastor Atoche's body was left in the operating room for a little over an hour. His loved ones were broken, crying at the death of their father, pastor, and leader. It was a very painful time of grief.

While this was occurring, Pastor Guillermo Maldonado was in Dallas, Texas—over 3,200 miles away—doing a telethon for Enlace, a TBN affiliate. Pastor Atoche's wife had sent an offering to Enlace, and it was Pastor Maldonado's turn to touch and pray for the offerings that had been called in. He had no idea what was happening to this pastor, but the Lord showed him something, and, in obedience, he gave this order: "Rise! In the name of Jesus, I order you to rise!" At that precise moment, Pastor Atoche came back to life—he resurrected! Imagine the commotion in the hospital! This is the power of the resurrection in Christ. God raised him from clinical death, and he went on to live with a perfectly healthy heart. Today, Pastor Atoche is an exceptional witness of what it means to move in the glory of God. He prays for the sick, and the power of the resurrection continues to manifest through him in Peru, healing, delivering, saving, and restoring life. The latter glory is manifesting!

Study 16

Manifesting God's Glory as You Go

"Go into all the world and preach the gospel to every creature."
—Mark 16:15

Introduction

Will you carry the presence and glory of God everywhere you go, manifesting His works? In this final study, we will see how to step up to another level of passion and boldness that will compel us, through the love of Christ, to go out and win souls for Jesus, disciple believers, and be witnesses who manifest God's glory through miracles, healings, and other marvels. People of every race, culture, and socioeconomic status are being transformed into vessels that manifest His glory. Jesus said that signs would follow believers, and you are no exception! Allow God to manifest His presence in your life, to His honor and glory.

Study Questions

Part I: Called to Manifest God's Glory

1. What will God's people make known to the *"sons of men"*? (Psalm 145:12)

   _____

2. What did Jesus say would be some characteristics of those who believe in Him and minister in His name? (Mark 16:17b–18)

   _____

   _____

3. By what means can we accomplish the will of the Lord, and by what means can't we? (Zechariah 4:6b)

_____

_____

Believers are common people used by a supernatural God to do uncommon things.

Part II: A Glorious Church

4. How did Paul describe the church that Jesus will come for when He returns—the church He died for in order to sanctify and cleanse? (Ephesians 5:27)

_____

_____

REFLECTIONS ON CHRIST'S "GLORIOUS" CHURCH

The word *"glorious"* in reference to the church in Ephesians 5:27 indicates the manifestation of every aspect of the essence of God. Let us remember that the Hebrew word for "glory," *kabowd*, is used figuratively in the sense of "splendor," "abundance," "honor," or "glory." In the Old Testament, *kabowd* is used variously to describe an individual's wealth, power or majesty, influential position, or great honor.

Someone glorious is honorable, illustrious, esteemed, wealthy, solvent, secure, of high reputation, and splendid. Accordingly, a glorious church is one that visibly demonstrates the power of God with miracles, signs, wonders, healings, and the casting out of demons. A glorious church manifests the holiness, character, and purity of its King; it manifests His wealth on earth. It shines with the light of Christ, testifying of Him wherever it goes and removing the darkness. This glorious church continually preaches, establishes, and expands the kingdom everywhere. It manifests the resurrection life of Jesus by doing creative miracles, by raising the dead, and by taking dominion in every area of society—politics, science, medicine, business, sports, education, religion, the arts, and more—by shining the light of Christ and dispelling the darkness of Satan.

The end-time movement of God will be a movement of the manifestations of the sons of God.

5. (a) Although we undergo various types of pain and suffering in this world, what are these things not worthy to be compared with? (Romans 8:18)

_____

(b) For what does the creation wait with eager and earnest expectation? (Verse 19)

_____

6. Recall the effect that persecutions and trials "work" for us. (2 Corinthians 4:17b)

_____

7. No matter what we undergo, what are we through Christ and His love? (Romans 8:37)

_____

The believer who wants to be a vessel chosen to carry the glory of God must cross over the lines of comfort, convenience, and natural reason.

Part III: Demonstrating the Kingdom, Power, and Glory

8. (a) What did Jesus say belongs to God the Father? (Matthew 6:13b)

_____

(b) Recall what we are to pray to God regarding His kingdom. (Verse 10)

_____

REFLECTIONS ON THE KINGDOM, POWER, AND GLORY

Each of these aspects is distinct: The kingdom is the message of heaven. The power is the ability of heaven. And the glory is the atmosphere or environment of heaven. Jesus powerfully demonstrated the message of the gospel He carried and brought the environment of heaven to earth. We are called to do the same. The main reason believers who have been baptized in the Holy Spirit and with fire attend church is to receive knowledge, revelation, activation, and the fire of His glory to take it "all" out there. If the kingdom is not being manifested in the streets, and if the knowledge of the glory is not filling the earth, it is because many believers are not doing anything with what they have received.

---

9. In what two distinct actions was Jesus continually engaged while He ministered on earth? (Acts 1:1b)

   _____

10. What reason did Nicodemus give for his conclusion that Jesus was a teacher who had come from God? (John 3:2b)

   _____

New Testament believers should teach, demonstrate, and flow in the supernatural.

---

11. In what manner did Jesus say the kingdom of God had been advancing since the days of John the Baptist? (Matthew 11:12 NIV)

   _____

12. (a) In what way did Paul communicate the gospel message to the Corinthians? (1 Corinthians 2:4b)

   _____

   (b) In what way was his message *not* communicated? (Verse 4a)

   _____

   (c) What was Paul's aim in communicating the gospel in the manner he did? (Verse 5)

   _____

The supernatural was designed to be first experienced and then understood.

Part IV: Steps to Manifest the Glory of God Today

13. The first step to manifest the glory of God is to believe wholeheartedly. Recall what Jesus told Martha she would see if she believed. (John 11:40)

    _____

14. The second step is to make yourself available to God for the purposes of His glory. Recall what Isaiah replied when God asked, *"Who will go for Us?"* (Isaiah 6:8b)

    _____

15. The third step is to commit to go and manifest the glory of God.

    (a) What commission did Jesus give to His disciples just before He ascended to heaven? (Mark 16:15)

    _____

    (b) In what places did Jesus say His disciples would be witnesses to Him? (Acts 1:8)

    _____

KEY DEFINITION: The word *"go"* in the phrase *"Go into all the world"* (Mark 16:15) is translated from the Greek word *poreuomai*, which means "to go on one's way, to proceed from one place to another"; it "is more distinctly used to indicate procedure or course."[1]

16. In what manner did the apostles begin to fulfill Jesus' commission as they gave witness to His resurrection in Jerusalem? (Acts 4:33a)

    _____

17. Jesus' followers preached the gospel in Jerusalem, where the church had been established. However, what did it take for many of them to move on to the regions of Judea and Samaria? (Acts 8:1)

    _____

---

1. *Vine's Complete Expository Dictionary of Old and New Testament Words* (Nashville, TN: Thomas Nelson, Inc., Publishers, 1985), 269, s.v. "Go (Went), Go Onward."

18. (a) In what way did Philip expand the ministry of the gospel in fulfillment of Christ's statement about where His followers would be witnesses to Him? (Acts 8:5)

    _____

    (b) How did he continue to expand the reach of the gospel? (Verse 40b)

    _____

19. (a) Whom did the Lord call to preach the gospel primarily to the Gentiles? (Acts 9:11, 15; 26:14b, 17)

    _____

    (b) To what peoples did this man preach the gospel in fulfillment of Jesus' commission? (Acts 26:20a)

    _____

    _____

You will experience the power and the glory of God only as you go.

REFLECTIONS ON "GOING INTO ALL THE WORLD"

The Greek word translated *"world"* in Mark 16:15 is *kosmos*, which means "orderly arrangement" or "world." In its immediate sense there, it apparently refers to the physical earth as the scene of human habitation,[2] since Mark used a present participle, "as you are going about into the world." Yet, in another sense, the word *kosmos* can denote "'the present condition of human affairs,' in alienation from and opposition to God." I consider that sense of *kosmos* (cosmos) to be the social order that is organized or structured in the world in which we live, and is designed to work against the system, government, or kingdom of God, because Satan is the *"ruler of this world"* (John 12:31). What are the systems of this world? The major systems are: political, judicial, artistic (theater, movies, music, and other entertainment), economic/financial, educational, communicational, medical, and religious. Even though there

---

2. See, for example, Watchman Nee, *Love Not the World: A Prophetic Call to Holy Living* (Fort Washington, PA: CLC Publications), 11.

are believers working in each of these areas, these systems are generally controlled by Satan and his human agents—people who serve him (knowingly or unknowingly) in maintaining the systems. We can "go" with God's power, kingdom, and presence to remove the demonic powers that control these systems, so that people will come to know Christ and so that those who belong to the kingdom of God can influence these areas.

Part V: Demonstrate the Supernatural as You "Go"

20. As we go to those who do not know Christ, what are we to do in addition to sharing the message of the gospel with them? (Matthew 10:8)

    _____

21. (a) Whom can we rely on to work with us as we preach the gospel, as was the case with the early Christians? (Mark 16:20)

    _____

    (b) Recall what God will use to confirm His word. (Verse 20b)

    _____

22. What did Paul ask the Thessalonians to pray on behalf of him and his ministry team, which we should also pray as we minister the gospel? Complete the following:

    2 Thessalonians 3:1: *"Pray for us,* _____ _____ _____ _____

    _____ _____ _____ _____ _____

    _____ _____ _____, *just as it is with you."*

**The only movement able to generate transformation in society
is the outpouring of the glory of God.**

Conclusion

When you spend time in God's presence and glory, you discover the true purpose for which you were created, and there is nothing more satisfying than that—your life finally makes sense. You live each day passionately, as you see the supernatural power of God flow through your lips and hands.

Most of the time, Jesus demonstrated before He taught. The supernatural demonstration makes people's hearts receptive to believe and receive the Word. You can join the "new wine" generation of men and women whom God is raising up to demonstrate His glory, whose mission is to impact cities, nations, and continents. You can become an instrument that God will use in releasing the greatest flow of miracles the world has ever seen and to gather the final harvest of souls.

Each chapter in the book of Acts was written for you to receive knowledge and revelation, impartation and activation, so that you could immediately go and do the same. The moment you learn something, you become responsible before God to practice it. If you merely convert it to head knowledge, you will become one more religious person who knows truth but does not live it. Therefore, before this happens, or even if it has already happened, I challenge you to make the decision to go to your "world"—your home, office, business, and city—and testify of Jesus. I assure you that the glory of God will manifest with unquestionable signs, because this is the time for the manifestation of the glory in and through believers. The signs follow those who go and obey, according to the Word of God. Become God's instrument as a carrier of His presence and manifest His glory as you go!

Prayer of Activation

Father of glory, we will make known in the world Your mighty acts and the glorious majesty of Your kingdom. Empower us to go to others in demonstration of the Spirit and power, so that the people who come to faith in Jesus can build their faith on Your power and not on man's wisdom. People all over the world need to know that You are real, and they need Your Presence in their lives so they may be transformed spiritually, physically, emotionally, mentally, and socially. Someone must go to them with Your presence and glory. Here we are, Lord—send us! In the name of Jesus, amen.

Action Steps

+ If you have never received Christ as your Savior and Lord, take the opportunity to do so right now. Only if you have a relationship with the heavenly Father will you be able to reflect His glory and take that glory to the world. Repeat this prayer:

Heavenly Father, I recognize that I am a sinner, and now I repent of all my sins. With my mouth I confess that Jesus is the Son of God, and I believe in my heart that the Father raised Him from the dead. In the name of Jesus, I am saved. Amen!

+ As you go out to your "world," tell others the gospel of Jesus Christ, asking God to confirm His Word through you with accompanying signs of healings and miracles. These things will take place when we forget about ourselves and become centered on others. When you wake up in the morning, ask God to place across your path someone in need—someone who is sick, depressed, or lost. Ask Him for boldness to manifest His presence so that person can see His glorious light and be saved and delivered.

EXPERIENCES WITH GOD'S GLORY

A Genetic Disorder That Produced Dwarfism Healed

Matias was born with achondroplasia, which is a genetic disorder that results in dwarfism. The doctors explained to Matias's mother that a lack of amniotic fluid had stunted her son's growth in the womb. The medical resources in the area where they lived were limited. Even so, they consulted several doctors, but none could give them any hope. Matias was unable to rotate his arms. He also could not walk steadily, and he underwent surgery to correct the curvature in his legs—they were in danger of crossing over into an X—but without positive results.

This young man was also dealing with severe guilt and low self-esteem because he considered himself a burden to his parents. He sought relief in alcohol and drugs, and he stopped going to school because he felt rejected by his fellow students. At the age of twenty-one, he was still no taller than a ten-year-old boy. He desperately needed a miracle!

Then, Matias attended one of King Jesus Ministry's healing services in Argentina, where he lives. After Pastor Guillermo Maldonado declared a word for creative miracles, Matias came forward to testify. He said he felt the fire of God touch him, and he was able to move his arms normally. Matias cried so much, it was plain to see that the powerful presence of God was upon him. When Pastor Maldonado saw how small he was, his heart was moved with compassion, and the Holy Spirit guided him to declare that in twenty-four hours, his body would begin to grow. Then, Matias fell under the power of God.

Pastor Maldonado returned home, but, the following day, Matias's pastor—who is also a doctor—called to tell him that Matias was growing! He had grown a little over two centimeters (about three quarters of an inch) in the first twenty-four hours. Forty-eight hours later, he had grown three more centimeters (a little more than an inch); seventy-two hours later, three additional centimeters. He grew until his clothing no longer fit him properly. In three days, he grew a total of eight centimeters (a little more than three inches)! And he continues to grow.

Matias started to complain of muscle aches—especially in the muscles between his hips and legs, as well as his quadriceps—so he returned to the doctor to see what was happening. The doctor explained that since his bones had grown so much, all of his muscles, tendons, tissues, and so forth had to adjust accordingly. This miracle transformed the life of a young man, his family, and all who know him. Matias returned to school, and he shares his testimony everywhere he goes, using it to increase the faith of others, who also need healing. What happened to him was impossible in the natural, but it was possible in the glory of God.

ANSWER KEY

Study 1: Our Glorious God

Part I: God's Glory Fills Heaven and Earth

1. the greatness; the power and the glory; the victory and the majesty; all that is in heaven and in earth; the kingdom

2. *"Alleluia! Salvation and glory and honor and power belong to the Lord our God!"*

3. above the heavens

4. (a) the glory of God; (b) His handiwork; (c) *"There is no speech nor language where their voice is not heard. Their line has gone out through all the earth, and their words to the end of the world."*

5. God's righteousness

6. the whole earth

7. No.

8. the glorious splendor of God's majesty and His wondrous works

Part II: To God Be the Glory

9. *"Holy, holy, holy is the Lord of hosts."*

10. *"My glory I will not give to another, nor My praise to carved images."*

11. (a) his wisdom; (b) his might; (c) his riches

12. that he understands and knows that God is the Lord; the Lord Himself

13. lovingkindness, judgment, and righteousness in the earth

Part III: God Shares His Glory

14. God humbles Himself to behold the things that are in the heavens and in the earth.

15. (d)

16. the Father of glory

17. bringing many sons to glory

18. the glory that the Father had given Him

19. the Spirit

Study 2: You Are Made for Glory

Part I: Life Within God's Glory

1. God

2. (a) dry land, or Earth; (b) the waters, or Seas; (c) grass; herbs and their seed; fruit trees that yield fruit according to their kinds and contain their own seeds

3. (a) the dust of the ground; (b) He breathed into his nostrils the breath of life. (c) He made her out of one of the man's ribs.

4. God's

5. Spirit

6. the spirit

7. those who worship Him in spirit and truth

8. (a) crowned him with glory and honor; (b) made him to have dominion; put all things under his feet

9. (a) planted a garden; (b) trees that were pleasing to the sight and good for food; the tree of life; the tree of the knowledge of good and evil; a river to water the garden; (c) The Lord God put him there.

10. (a) the Lord God's; (b) heard the sound of the Lord God

Part II: Life Outside God's Glory

11. "Of every tree of the garden you may freely eat; but of the tree of the knowledge of good and evil you shall not eat, for in the day that you eat of it you shall surely die."

12. (a) Eve ate fruit from the tree of the knowledge of good and evil, and she gave some to Adam, who ate it also. (b) She saw that the tree was good for food, pleasant to the eyes, and desirable to make one wise.

13. (a) He said that she would not die but that her eyes would be opened and she would be like God, knowing good and evil. (b) Yes. They had already been made in His image and likeness. (c) Yes.

14. (a) Their eyes were opened, and they knew they were naked. (b) They sewed coverings for themselves out of fig leaves. (c) They hid themselves from His presence among the trees of the garden.

15. dead in trespasses and sins

16. (a) sent him out of the garden of Eden; (b) drove out the man

17. cherubim and a flaming sword that turned in all directions

18. All have sinned and fall short of the glory of God.

19. "The glory has departed from Israel!"

20. "And I will put enmity between you and the woman, and between your seed and her Seed; He shall bruise your head, and you shall bruise His heel."

21. The house of Israel is depicted as "the vineyard of the Lord of hosts"; the men of Judah are depicted as God's "pleasant plant."

22. (a) the "true vine"; (b) the "gardener"

23. (a) the *"branches"*; (b) *"much fruit"*

24. (a) watered garden; spring of water; waters do not fail; (b) *"He who believes in Me, as the Scripture has said, out of his heart will flow rivers of living water."*

Study 3: The Lord of Glory Came to Earth

Part I: Jesus' Glory in Eternity

1. with the glory that He had with the Father before the world existed

2. (a) before the foundation of the world; (b) in these last times for you who through Him believe in God; (c) He raised Him from the dead and gave Him glory.

3. the Lord of glory

Part II: Jesus' Glory on Earth

4. (a) Glory; (b) peace, goodwill

5. glorious

6. honor and glory

7. *"'Blessed is the King who comes in the name of the LORD!' Peace in heaven and glory in the highest!"*

8. *"Now the Son of Man is glorified, and God is glorified in Him."*

9. (c)

10. (a) He had glorified the Father on the earth. (b) He finished the work that God had given Him to do.

Part III: Jesus' Glory Given to Men

11. glory and honor

12. received up in glory

13. (a) authority over all flesh; for the purpose of giving eternal life to as many as the Father has given Him; (b) to know the only true God and Jesus Christ whom He has sent

14. (a) the glory that the Father had given Him; (b) that they may be with Him where He is, and that they may behold the glory He received from the Father

15. wisdom from God; righteousness; sanctification; redemption

16. ours

17. bringing them to glory

18. to give us the light of the knowledge of His glory in the face of Jesus Christ

19. should shine on them

20. *"But we have this treasure in earthen vessels, that the excellence of the power may be of God and not of us."*

21. *"He who glories, let him glory in the LORD."*

22. Christ in you

23. what is the hope of God's calling, the riches of the glory of His inheritance in the saints, and the exceeding greatness of His power toward us who believe

Study 4: The Manifest Presence of God

Part I: Manifestations in the Old Testament

1. The God of glory appeared to our father Abraham

2. (a) The angel of the Lord appeared to Moses in a flame of fire from the mist of a bush that was burning with fire but not consumed. (b) to bring His people, the children of Israel, out of Egypt

3. (a) a pillar of cloud by day and a pillar of fire by night; (b) The pillar of cloud led the way by day, and the pillar of fire gave them light at night, so they could travel by day or night. (c) The cloud covered the tabernacle of meeting, and the glory of the Lord filled the tabernacle. (d) When the cloud was taken up from above the tabernacle, the Israelites would move forward, but if the cloud was not taken up, they did not journey.

4. It served as a covering.

5. (a) thunder and lightning, a thick cloud on the mountain, and the loud sound of a trumpet; (b) It was completely covered in smoke; the smoke ascended like the smoke of a furnace, and the whole mountain quaked greatly. It looked that way because the Lord had descended on it in fire. (c) *"by voice"*

6. Under God's feet was what looked like pavement made out of sapphire stone that was *"like the very heavens"* in its clearness.

7. (a) from above the mercy seat and between the two cherubim on the ark of the Testimony; (b) between the cherubim

8. (a) *"Please, show me Your glory."* (b) God told Moses He would make all His goodness pass before him and would proclaim the name of the Lord before Him, but Moses could see only His back, not His face.

9. It shone.

10. (a) The glory of the Lord filled the house of God in the form of a cloud that was so powerful the priests could not stand to minister. (b) Fire came down from heaven and consumed the burnt offering and the sacrifices; the glory of the Lord filled the temple. (c) They bowed down to the ground and worshipped and praised the Lord, saying, *"For He is good, for His mercy endures forever."* Then, they offered sacrifices to the Lord.

11. (a) a great and strong wind that tore into the mountains and broke the rocks in pieces, an earthquake, and a fire; (b) No. (c) in a *"still small voice"*; (d) He wrapped his face in his mantle.

12. A chariot of fire appeared with horses of fire, and Elijah went up into heaven by a whirlwind.

13. (a) He was high and lifted up, and the train of His robe filled the temple. (b) seraphim; (c) *"Holy, holy, holy is the* Lord *of hosts; the whole earth is full of His glory!"* (d) The posts of the door were shaken, and the temple was filled with smoke.

14. (a) *"Woe is me, for I am undone! Because I am a man of unclean lips, and I dwell in the midst of a people of unclean lips; for my eyes have seen the King, the* Lord *of hosts."* (b) One of the seraphim touched

Isaiah's mouth with a live coal, which he had taken with tongs from the altar, and said, *"Behold, this has touched your lips; Your iniquity is taken away, and your sin purged."* (c) The Lord said, *"Whom shall I send, and who will go for Us?"* Isaiah replied, *"Here am I! Send me."*

15. (a) He said it was like a sapphire stone. (b) a likeness with the appearance of a man; (c) From His waist upward, the *"man"* was the color of amber with the appearance of fire all around within it, and from His waist downward there was the appearance of fire with brightness all around. The brightness looked like a rainbow in a cloud on a rainy day.

16. (a) the likeness of the glory of the Lord; (b) He fell on his face, and he heard a voice of One speaking. (c) to send him to the rebellious, impudent, and stubborn Israelites, to give them the word of the Lord

17. a great thunderous voice, saying, *"Blessed is the glory of the LORD from His place!"*; the noise of the wings of the living creatures that touched one another; the noise of the wheels beside them; a great thunderous noise

Part II: Manifestations in the New Testament

18. It shone around them.

19. (a) He saw the heavens open and the Spirit of God descending like a dove and alighting upon Him. He heard a voice from heaven saying, *"This is My beloved Son, in whom I am well pleased."* (b) He descended in bodily form.

20. (a) The appearance of His face was altered; His face shone like the sun, and His robe, or clothes, became as white as light, and glistened. (b) *"His clothes became shining, exceedingly white, like snow, such as no launderer on earth can whiten them."* (c) Moses and Elijah; (d) in glory; (e) He manifested Himself to them through a bright cloud that overshadowed them, and by speaking to them from the cloud. He told them, *"This is My beloved Son, in whom I am well pleased. Hear Him!"*

21. (a) There was a sound from heaven, like a rushing mighty wind, which filled the whole house where they were sitting. Then, *"divided tongues"* appeared to them, resembling fire, and one *"tongue"* rested upon each of them. (b) speaking with *"other tongues,"* as the Spirit gave them utterance; (c) *"the wonderful works of God"*

22. (a) the glory of God, and Jesus standing at the right hand of God; (b) being full of the Holy Spirit

23. (a) A light from heaven suddenly shone around him. He fell to the ground, and he heard a voice saying, *"Saul, Saul, why are you persecuting Me?"* (b) He was blind for three days. (c) Something like scales fell from his eyes, and he received his sight. (d) He would be filled with the Holy Spirit. (e) He arose and was baptized. (f) to be a chosen vessel of the Lord to bear His name before Gentiles, kings, and the children of Israel

24. (a) an earthquake that caused the foundations of the prison to be shaken, all the prison doors to be opened, and all the prisoners' chains to be loosed; (b) He and all his family believed in God and were baptized; the jailer rejoiced.

25. (a) He was clothed with a garment down to His feet and had a golden band around His chest. His head and hair were white, like wool or snow, and His eyes were like a flame of fire. His feet were like fine brass. (b) the sound of many waters; (c) He had seven stars in His right hand, and out of His mouth came a sharp two-edged sword. (d) *"like the sun shining in its strength"*; (e) The temple was filled with smoke from the glory and power of God.

Study 5: Natural Knowledge and Revealed Knowledge

Part I: Helpful Lessons from the Natural World

1. (a) the glory of God; (b) through all the earth, to the end of the world; (c) God's invisible attributes; (d) His eternal power and Godhead

2. (a) The ant, having no captain, overseer, or ruler, provides supplies for itself in the summer and gathers its food in the harvest. (b) Poverty may come upon us like a prowler, and need like an armed man.

3. (a) It is smaller than all the other seeds on earth, but after it is sown, it grows and becomes greater than all herbs, shooting out large branches, so that the birds of the air may nest under its shade. (b) whatever he sows; (c) If we sow to the flesh, we will reap corruption; if we sow to the Spirit, we will reap everlasting life.

4. (a) *"Arise and go down to the potter's house…"*; (b) A potter was making a clay vessel at his wheel, but the vessel was marred, so he made it into another vessel, as seemed good to him. (c) clay; potter's hand; you in My hand

5. (a) *"There are still four months and then comes the harvest."* (b) *"…lift up your eyes and look at the fields, for they are already white for harvest!"* (c) *"When you see a cloud rising in the west, immediately you say, 'It's going to rain,' and it does. And when the south wind blows, you say, 'It's going to be hot,' and it is."* (d) He told them that they knew how to interpret the appearance of the earth and the sky, so why didn't they know how to interpret the present time?

Part II: Limitations of Natural Knowledge

6. (a) They ate fruit from the tree of the knowledge of good and evil. (b) the knowledge that they were naked; (c) knowledge of the physical realm

7. (a) *"That which is born of the flesh is flesh, and that which is born of the Spirit is spirit."* (b) water and the Spirit

8. (a) No. (b) through revelation by God's Spirit; (c) They have received the Spirit who is from God; they have not received the spirit of the world.

Part III: Consequences of a Lack of Revealed Knowledge

9. a return to "dust," or death

10. To be carnally minded is death; to be spiritually minded is life and peace.

11. (a) changed their Glory for what does not profit; (b) the fountain of living waters; (c) broken cisterns that could hold no water

12. (a) They can become futile in their thoughts, and their foolish hearts can be darkened. (b) an image made like corruptible man, as well as like birds, four-footed animals, and creeping things; (c) the lie; (d) a debased mind; (e) uncleanness, in the lusts of their hearts, which leads to dishonoring their bodies among themselves

13. The word of the Lord was rare; there was no widespread revelation.

14. (a) They cast off restraint. (b) They perish.

15. God's people are destroyed for lack of knowledge.

Part IV: Man's Knowledge Versus God's Knowledge

16. (a) lean on our own understanding or be wise in our own eyes; (b) trust in the Lord with all our hearts and acknowledge Him in all our ways; (c) direct our paths

17. Because its end is the way of death.

18. (a) foolishness with God; (b) that they are futile

19. (a) *"as the heavens are higher than the earth"*; (b) *"Why do you spend money for what is not bread, and your wages for what does not satisfy?"* (c) Listen carefully to Me; (d) They will live. (e) He must forsake his way and his thoughts.

20. (a) by inspiration of God; (b) Holy men of God spoke as they were moved by the Holy Spirit. (c) the will of man

Part V: Revealed Knowledge

21. (a) Jesus told him that His Father in heaven had revealed it to him. (b) flesh and blood

22. signs and wonders, various miracles, and gifts of the Holy Spirit

23. (a) my gospel and the preaching of Jesus Christ; revelation of the mystery; made manifest; (b) revealed by the Spirit; apostles; prophets

24. the word of wisdom; the word of knowledge; prophecy; the interpretation of tongues

25. (a) that they may prophesy; (b) edification, exhortation, and comfort

26. dream dreams; see visions

27. He would guide them into all truth. Whatever He heard, He would speak, and He would tell them things to come.

28. *"The things which are impossible with men are possible with God."*

Study 6: From Foundational Doctrine to Revelation

Part I: Build a Foundation of Basic Doctrine

1. (a) the Holy Scriptures; (b) salvation through faith in Christ Jesus

2. (a) It is profitable for doctrine, reproof, correction, and instruction in righteousness. (b) every good work

3. the pure milk of the word, in order to grow

4. (a) We will be unskilled in the word of righteousness; we will remain "babies." (b) *"those who are of full age, that is, those who by reason of use have their senses exercised to discern both good and evil"*

5. We should leave the discussion of the elementary principles of Christ, and we should go on to perfection.

Part II: Live What You Know

6. (b)

7. (a) a wise man who built his house on the rock; (b) heavy rain and floods; fierce winds; (c) founded

8. (a) They have no root. (b) They bring no fruit to maturity. (c) They "keep" the Word, and they bear fruit with patience.

9. love, joy, peace, longsuffering, kindness, goodness, faithfulness, gentleness, self-control

10. (a) virtue; (b) knowledge, self-control, perseverance, godliness, brotherly kindness, and love; (c) being barren and unfruitful in the knowledge of our Lord Jesus Christ

Part III: Go "from Faith to Faith"

11. from faith to faith

12. *"For as the body without the spirit is dead, so faith without works is dead also."*

13. much will be required; of him they will ask the more

14. power

15. through accompanying signs

16. many signs and wonders

17. Unclean spirits came out of those who were possessed; many who were paralyzed and lame were healed.

18. so that the Corinthians' faith would not be in the wisdom of men but in the power of God

19. faith, gifts of healings, the working of miracles, the discerning of spirits, and different kinds of tongues

Part IV: Seek Fresh Revelation

20. (a) a great famine that would be throughout the world; (b) Each disciple, according to his ability, donated to a relief collection on behalf of the believers in Judea; they enlisted Barnabas and Saul to take the relief to the elders of the church in that region.

21. (a) to separate to Him Barnabas and Saul for the work to which He had called them; (b) ministering to the Lord and fasting

22. (a) *"For it seemed good to the Holy Spirit, and to us…."* (b) by revelation; (c) those who were of reputation

23. (a) They were forbidden by the Holy Spirit. (b) The Spirit did not permit them. (c) *"A man of Macedonia stood and pleaded with him, saying, 'Come over to Macedonia and help us.'"* (d) They concluded that the Lord had called them to preach the gospel to the Macedonians, so they sought to go to Macedonia.

Part V: Discern False Teachings and Manifestations

24. (a) Two or three prophets should speak, and the rest should judge what they say. We are not to believe every spirit, but we are to test them. (b) the prophets; (c) peace; (d) *"Let all things be done decently and in order."*

25. (a) *"hold fast what is good"*; (b) *"Do not quench the Spirit."* (c) to prophesy; (d) speaking in tongues

26. (a) He tempted Jesus to command stones to become bread. (b) He told the devil, *"It is written, 'Man shall not live by bread alone, but by every word that proceeds from the mouth of God.'"*

27. compassion

28. selfish ambition; love

29. (a) money; (b) Simon was poisoned by bitterness and bound by iniquity.

30. (a) wants to do His; will; (b) his own glory; (c) the glory of the One who sent Him

Study 7: Three Dimensions of the Supernatural

Part I: Faith

1. a measure of faith

2. *"Faith is the substance of things hoped for, the evidence of things not seen."*

3. we walk by faith

4. (a) We do not look at the things that are seen, and we look at the things that are unseen. (b) The things that are seen are temporary, but the things that are unseen are eternal.

5. Without faith, it is impossible to please God.

6. (a) that we receive them; (b) We will have what we asked for.

7. faith in God

8. by faith in the Son of God

9. *"But the just shall live by his faith."*

Part II: Anointing

10. The Spirit of the Lord came upon him from that day forward.

11. an endowment in wisdom, understanding, knowledge, and in all manner of workmanship, to design artistic works and to work in gold, silver, and bronze; to cut jewels for setting and to carve wood

12. an anointing from the Holy One

13. (a) He said they would be baptized with the Holy Spirit. (b) power; (c) They were filled with the Holy Spirit and began to speak with other tongues as the Spirit gave them utterance.

14. (a) They laid hands on the Samaritans, and the Samaritans received the Holy Spirit. (b) The Holy Spirit fell upon them. (c) They spoke with tongues and magnified God. (d) He laid hands on them. (e) The Holy Spirit came upon them, and they spoke with tongues and prophesied.

15. (a) manifestation of the Spirit is given; for the profit of all; (b) distributing to each one individually as He wills

16. (a) apostle, prophet, evangelist, pastor, and teacher; (b) for equipping the saints for the work of ministry, and for edifying the body of Christ

17. They fasted and prayed; then, they laid hands on Paul and Barnabas and sent them away.

18. (a) They anointed them with oil. (b) A believer who is sick should call for the elders of the church and let them pray over him, anointing him with oil in the name of the Lord. (c) the prayer of faith; (d) He will be forgiven.

19. (a) power going out from Me; (b) her faith

20. Jesus was anointed to preach the gospel to the poor, to heal the brokenhearted, to proclaim liberty to the captives and recovery of sight to the blind, to set at liberty those who are oppressed, and to proclaim the acceptable year of the Lord.

21. (a) the Holy Spirit and power; (b) He went about doing good and healing all who were oppressed by the devil.

22. They would do the works that He did, and even greater works, because He was going to the Father.

Part III: Glory

23. (a) for God took him; (b) It says that he walked with God.

24. The cloud covered the tabernacle, and the glory of the Lord filled the tabernacle.

25. (a) The fire of the Lord fell and consumed the sacrifice, the wood, the stones, and the dust, and it licked up the water in the trench. (b) They fell on their faces, saying, "The Lord, He is God! The Lord, He is God!"

26. (a) It says that the Midianites, Amalekites, and *"people of the East"* were *"as numerous as locusts"* and that their camels were *"as the sand by the seashore in multitude."* (b) three hundred; (c) trumpets and empty pitchers with torches inside of them; (d) They blew the trumpets and broke the pitchers; they held the torches in their left hands and the trumpets in their right hands. (e) *"The sword of the Lord and of Gideon!"* (f) The whole army cried out and fled.

27. (a) The Holy Spirit would come upon her, and the power of the Highest would overshadow her. (b) *"Behold the maidservant of the Lord! Let it be to me according to your word."*

28. (a) four days; (b) *"Did I not say to you that if you would believe you would see the glory of God?"* (c) Lazarus came out of the tomb alive. (d) He should be loosed from his graveclothes and be let go.

29. (a) three thousand; (b) five thousand

30. powers of the age to come

Study 8: Transitioning from the Anointing to the Glory

Part I: Who Receives Revelation?

1. (a) those who fear Him; show them His covenant; (b) us and to our children forever; do all the words of this law

2. His Spirit

3. He would answer him and show him great and mighty things that he did not know.

4. the spirit of wisdom and revelation in the knowledge of Him

212 The Glory of God

Part II: Jesus Opened the Way to Ongoing Revelation

5. It was torn in two from top to bottom.

6. (a) having become High Priest forever; (b) His own blood; (c) once for all

7. the Presence

8. (a) with boldness; by the blood of Jesus; (b) with a true heart in full assurance of faith

9. hope of the glory of God

Part III: Develop a New Mind-set

10. *"I will put My laws into their hearts, and in their minds I will write them."*

11. our heart, our soul, and our mind

12. things above

13. *"Your kingdom come. Your will be done on earth as it is in heaven."*

14. all things

Part IV: Allow God to Be God

15. (a) Be still, and know that He is God. (b) among the nations and in the earth

16. (a) God the Father's; (b) because He loves the Son

17. (a) *"Not as I will, but as You will."* (b) deny ourselves, take up our cross, and follow Jesus; (c) Those who desire to save their lives will lose them, and those who lose their lives for Christ's sake will find them.

18. the things that He suffered

19. (a) made Himself of no reputation; (b) humbled Himself; became obedient to the point of death

Part V: Respect the Glory

20. (a) He put out his hand and took hold of the ark. (b) He struck him dead, because he was in error.

21. (a) *"Is not this great Babylon, that I have built for a royal dwelling by my mighty power and for the honor of my majesty?"* (b) His kingdom would be taken away from him, and he would be driven from men and dwell with the beasts of the field, eating grass like oxen. (c) The Most High rules in the kingdom of men and gives rule to whomever He chooses. (d) put them down; (e) the Most High; because His dominion is an everlasting dominion, and His kingdom is from generation to generation

22. (a) *"The voice of a god and not of a man!"* (b) He was struck dead by an angel of the Lord, and worms ate him, because he did not give glory to God.

23. They lied to the Holy Spirit, and they tested the Spirit of the Lord.

24. (a) No. (b) *"This is My beloved Son. Hear Him!"*

Part VI: Revelation Comes to Those Who Hunger and Thirst

25. The Father will love him, and the Father and Jesus will come to him and make Their home with him.

26. those who hunger and thirst for righteousness

27. (a) to know the mysteries of the kingdom of heaven; (b) Their hearts have grown dull, their ears are hard of hearing, and they have closed their eyes. (c) because their eyes saw, and their ears heard

Study 9: A Passion to Seek God's Presence

Part I: Moses' Longing for God's Presence

1. (a) They trembled and stood afar off. (b) They said they wanted Moses to speak with them, and they would hear, but they didn't want God to speak with them, because they would "die." (c) He told them not to fear because God was testing them and wanted His "fear" to be before them so they would not sin. (d) He drew close to the thick darkness where God was.

2. (a) *"My Presence will go with you, and I will give you rest."* (b) *"I will also do this thing that you have spoken."* (c) Because Moses had found grace in His sight, and He knew him by name.

3. (a) face-to-face, as to a friend; plainly; (b) Moses was faithful in all God's house.

4. (a) that He might instruct them; (b) lest they act corruptly and make for themselves a carved image in any form; (c) to see God's glory

Part II: David's Zeal for God

5. a man after His own heart

6. (a) *"I have set the LORD always before me."* (b) fullness of joy and pleasures forevermore

7. the habitation of the Lord's house, and the place where His glory dwells

8. (a) that he might dwell in the house of the Lord all the days of his life; (b) to behold the beauty of the Lord and to inquire in His temple; (c) *"Your face, LORD, I will seek."*

9. (a) early; (b) *"My soul thirsts for You; my flesh longs for You in a dry and thirsty land where there is no water."* (c) in the sanctuary; (d) God's power and glory; (e) during the night

10. (a) He danced before the Lord with all his might. (b) leaping and whirling

Part III: Paul's Intense Desire for Intimacy with Christ

11. Christ and the power of His resurrection and the fellowship of His sufferings

12. (a) all things; (b) that I may gain Christ and be found in Him

13. (a) eagerly wait; (b) loved His appearing

14. its width, length, depth, and height

Part IV: Thirsting for God

15. (a) broken cisterns that couldn't hold water; (b) the fountain of living waters

16. (a) the living God; (b) *"As the deer pants for the water brooks, so pants my soul for You, O God."*

17. let him come to Me and drink

18. (a) Out of their hearts will flow rivers of living water. (b) the Holy Spirit

Part V: A Passion for God Leads to Revealed Knowledge

19. (a) just and devout; (b) the Consolation of Israel; (c) the Holy Spirit; (d) that he would not die before he had seen the Lord's Christ; (e) the Spirit's; (f) *"Lord, now You are letting Your servant depart in peace, according to Your word."*

20. (a) as a chief tax collector who was rich; (b) He climbed a sycamore tree. (c) *"Zacchaeus, make haste and come down, for today I must stay at your house."* (d) salvation has come to this house; (e) that if anyone loves Jesus, he will keep His Word, and the Father will love him, and the Father and Jesus will come to him and make Their home with him

21. (a) He will never thirst. (b) a fountain of water springing up into everlasting life; (c) *"God is Spirit, and those who worship Him must worship in spirit and truth."*

Part VI: Develop a Passion for God

22. by loving Him with all our heart, soul, and mind

23. His love for us

24. (a) an everlasting love; (b) He has drawn them with lovingkindness.

25. (a) He would spit them out of His mouth. (b) *"Be zealous and repent."* (c) merciful and gracious, slow to anger, and abounding in mercy

26. (a) while He may be found, and while He is near; (b) He will have mercy on us and abundantly pardon us.

27. (a) *"Whom have I in heaven but You? And there is none upon earth that I desire besides You."* (b) the strength of our heart and our portion forever

Study 10: Conditions, Rewards, and Benefits of the Glory

Part I: Four Conditions for Receiving God's Blessings

1. They had to humble themselves.

2. We must be converted and become as little children.

3. He will lift us up.

4. pray

5. He would return to them.

6. the Spirit of grace and supplication

7. He makes intercession for us with groanings that cannot be uttered; He makes intercession for the saints according to the will of God.

8. It avails much.

9. to seek His face

10. They would find Him.

11. to know the only true God, and Jesus Christ whom He has sent

12. They had to turn from their wicked ways.

13. (a) in returning and rest; (b) repentance leading to salvation; (c) death

14. (a) Whoever has two tunics should give one to someone who has none; whoever has food should share it with someone who has none. (b) Do not collect any more money than what is appointed for you to collect. (c) Do not intimidate anyone or falsely accuse him, and be content with your wages.

15. (a) their first love; (b) to remember from where they had fallen, to repent, and to do the *"first works"*

Part II: Three Results of Seeking God

16. a rewarder

17. He would hear from heaven.

18. (a) God had heard his voice and his supplications. (b) because He had inclined His ear to him

19. (a) If we ask anything according to His will, He hears us. (b) that we have the petitions we have asked of Him

20. He would forgive their sin.

21. God is faithful and just to forgive our sins and to cleanse us from all unrighteousness.

22. as far as the east is from the west

23. He would heal their land.

24. any good thing

25. He forgave all his iniquities, healed all his diseases, redeemed his life from destruction, crowned him with lovingkindness and tender mercies, and satisfied his mouth with good things, so that his youth was renewed like the eagle's.

Part III: We Must Seek God's Glory "Until…"

26. (a) We must sow for ourselves righteousness, and we must break up our fallow ground. (b) mercy; (c) until; (d) The Lord will come and rain righteousness on us.

27. *"Ask, and it will be given to you; seek, and you will find; knock, and it will be opened to you."*

28. with all his heart

29. We will reap in due season.

Study 11: Transformed into His Glory

Part I: From Glory to Glory

1. *"like the shining sun, that shines ever brighter unto the perfect day."*

2. (a) We are transformed into the image of the Lord, from glory to glory. (b) the Spirit of the Lord; (c) liberty; (d) being

3. that we might become the righteousness of God in Him

4. (a) that for which Christ Jesus had laid hold of him; (b) He forgot the things that were behind him, and he reached forward to the things that were ahead. (c) the goal for the prize of the upward call of God in Christ Jesus

5. (a) every weight and the sin that so easily ensnares us; (b) Jesus, the author and finisher of our faith

Part II: Renewal and Transformation

6. (a) the renewing of our minds; (b) what is the good, acceptable, and perfect will of God

7. this world

8. *"We ought to obey God rather than men."*

9. a bondservant of Christ

10. (a) in knowledge according to the image of Him who created him; (b) tender mercies, kindness, humility, meekness, and longsuffering; (c) We should bear with one another and forgive one another, even as Christ forgave us. (d) love

11. (a) It is being renewed day by day. (b) a far more exceeding and eternal weight of glory

12. (a) perseverance; (b) character and hope; (c) We are to glory in them. (d) drawing back

13. (a) the Spirit of glory and of God; (b) He is glorified.

Part III: Obstacles to Godly Transformation

14. rebellion; stubbornness

15. harden our hearts as in the rebellion

16. (a) its heart; (b) It was not faithful to God.

17. The fear of the Lord

18. pride

19. (a) shame; strife; being brought low; destruction; (b) being lifted up by the Lord; salvation; wisdom; honor; greatness in the kingdom of heaven; exaltation; grace

20. (a) He resists them. (b) grace; (c) He will exalt them in due time.

21. (a) We deceive ourselves. (b) the truth; (c) We make Him out to be a liar. (d) God's Word

22. (a) *"I am rich, have become wealthy, and have need of nothing."* (b) They were wretched, miserable, poor, blind, and naked.

23. *"Do not be wise in your own eyes; fear the LORD and depart from evil."*

24. (a) regulations; (b) the commandments and doctrines of men; (c) wisdom in self-imposed religion; false humility; neglect of the body; (d) not at all

25. (a) *"…these people draw near with their mouths and honor Me with their lips, but have removed their hearts far from Me."* (b) the commandment of men

26. (a) by grace and through faith; (b) ourselves; works; (c) It is the gift of God.

27. He has "wiped" it out; He has taken it out of the way, having nailed it to the cross.

28. denying its power

29. through the accompanying signs

Part IV: The Final Transformation in Glory

30. (a) The dead will be raised incorruptible, and those who are alive will be changed. (b) The corruptible will put on incorruption, and the mortal will put on immortality.

31. We will be like Him.

32. the day dawns and the morning star rises in your hearts

Study 12: Creating an Atmosphere to Bring His Presence, Part 1

Part I: The Lord Deserves Our Praise and Worship

1. glory, honor, and power; because He created all things, and by His will they exist

2. *"the Lord strong and mighty, the Lord mighty in battle"*

3. (a) in the praises of Israel; (b) He glorifies Him.

4. (a) with our whole heart; (b) from the rising of the sun until its going down; at all times; continually

Part II: Expressions of Praise

5. making a joyful shout; singing

6. (a) psalms, hymns, and spiritual songs; (b) by singing and making melody in our hearts to Him

7. clapping one's hands; lifting up one's hands

8. dancing

9. trumpet, lute, harp, timbrel, stringed instruments, flute, cymbals

Part III: Praise God Through Proclamation

10. (a) all His wondrous works; (b) the judgments of His mouth; (c) rejoice

11. (a) He made the heavens; He laid out the earth above the waters; He made the *"great lights"*—the sun, moon, and stars; He struck the firstborn of Egypt; He brought Israel out of Egypt; He divided the Red Sea and allowed Israel to pass through it; He overthrew Pharaoh and his army in the Red Sea; He led His people through the wilderness; He struck down great kings and slew famous kings and gave their land to the Israelites as a heritage; He remembered the Israelites in their lowly state and rescued them from their enemies; He gave food to all flesh. (b) His mercy, which endures forever

12. (a) the glorious splendor of God's majesty and His wondrous works; (b) the glory of His kingdom, and His power; (c) It is everlasting, enduring throughout all generations.

Part IV: Praise God Through Sacrifice

13. (a) the sacrifice of praise; (b) the fruit of our lips; giving thanks

14. the garment of praise

15. They had been stripped, beaten, and flogged, then thrown into prison, with their feet fastened in stocks.

16. There was a violent earthquake that shook the foundations of the prison, so that all the prison doors were opened and the chains of all the prisoners were loosened.

17. He and all his family believed in God and were baptized.

18. *"Rejoice and be exceedingly glad, for great is your reward in heaven."*

19. the glory due His name

Study 13: Creating an Atmosphere to Bring His Presence, Part 2

Part I: Honoring the Lord Through Worship

1. in the beauty of holiness

2. he who has clean hands and a pure heart

3. those who worship in spirit and truth

4. (a) ourselves; (b) the Lord's mercy and His truth

5. *"Now to the King eternal, immortal, invisible, to God who alone is wise, be honor and glory forever and ever. Amen."*

Part II: Revelations of True Worship

6. (a) your Maker is your Husband; (b) the bride, the Lamb's wife; (c) the glory of God

7. (a) His name; (b) all blessing and praise; (c) Jesus; (d) every knee should bow, and every tongue should confess that Jesus Christ is Lord; (e) glory

8. according to Your word

9. revealed

10. (a) *"Lord God of Israel, there is no God in heaven or on earth like You, who keep Your covenant and mercy with Your servants who walk before You with all their hearts."* (b) Fire came down from heaven and consumed the burnt offering and sacrifices, and the glory of the Lord filled the temple.

11. (a) *"Take up the ark of the covenant, and let seven priests bear seven trumpets of rams' horns before the ark of the Lord."* (b) They advanced and blew the trumpets. (c) The armed men marched ahead of the priests who blew the trumpets, and the rear guard came after the ark. (d) a great shout; (e) The wall fell down, and God's people went up into the city and took it.

12. (a) It was that of a rushing mighty wind. (b) the sounds of the disciples speaking with other tongues

13. (a) transformation into the image of Christ from glory to glory; (b) They will be like them.

Part III: Three Principles for Creating a Spiritual Atmosphere

14. in the praises of Israel

15. (a) the courts of the Lord; (b) the living God

16. (a) the glory of the Lord; (b) The Lord spoke to Moses.

17. *"Surely the Lord is in this place, and I did not know it."*

18. the Spirit who is from God
19. faith

Part IV: Responding to God's Glory

20. (a) *"How awesome is this place! This is none other than the house of God, and this is the gate of heaven!"* (b) He rose early, took the stone that he had used for a pillow, set it up as a pillar, and poured oil on top of it.
21. He instructed Moses to take off his sandals, because the place where he was standing was holy ground.
22. (a) *"Woe is me, for I am undone! Because I am a man of unclean lips, and I dwell in the midst of a people of unclean lips; for my eyes have seen the King, the Lord of hosts."* (b) *"Here am I! Send me."*
23. to heal and save him
24. (a) the power of the Lord; (b) No. (c) Jesus saw the faith of his friends. (d) They were all amazed, and they glorified God and were filled with fear.

Study 14: Ignited by the Fire of God

Part I: The Fire of God

1. (a) in a flame of fire from the midst of a bush that was burning with fire but not consumed; (b) from the midst of the bush
2. the pillar of fire
3. like a consuming fire
4. *"For the Lord your God is a consuming fire, a jealous God."*
5. walks righteously and speaks uprightly
6. *"Denying ungodliness and worldly lusts, we should live soberly, righteously, and godly in the present age."*
7. (a) sanctification; (b) sanctify them; (c) spirit, soul, and body; (d) He who called them, because He is faithful
8. Jesus Christ the righteous

Part II: Jesus Came to Bring Power and Fire

9. with the Holy Spirit and fire
10. fire
11. power from on high
12. They would be witnesses to Jesus in Jerusalem, in all Judea and Samaria, and to the end of the earth.
13. *"These who have turned the world upside down have come here too."*
14. He convicts the world of sin, of righteousness, and of judgment.

Part III: Ten Purposes of the Fire of God

15. (a) as *"the light of the world"*; (b) so that people may see our good works and glorify our Father in heaven

16. (a) The Lord rained brimstone and fire on them. (b) Fire went out from the Lord and devoured them, and they died before the Lord. (c) the heavens and the earth

17. (a) The Lord's judgment of His people is a chastening so that they may not be condemned with the world. (b) judging ourselves; (c) to search our hearts and to try us, in order to see if there is any wicked way in us, and to lead us in the way everlasting

18. (a) a refiner's fire and launderer's soap; (b) as a refiner and a purifier of silver; (c) that they may offer to the Lord an offering in righteousness

19. it is tested by fire

20. each person's work, of what sort it is

21. (a) like a burning fire shut up in my bones; (b) No.

22. (a) hostility from sinners against Himself; (b) hard work; floggings, including five instances of forty lashes minus one; imprisonment; exposure to death; beatings with rods; stoning; three shipwrecks, including the experience of being on the open sea for a night and a day; being frequently on the move; being in a variety of dangers, including those of rivers, of bandits, of his own countrymen, of the Gentiles, in the city, in the country, at sea, and from false brothers; laboring and toiling; frequent sleeplessness; hunger; thirst; going without food; being cold; being naked; and experiencing daily pressure due to his concern for all the churches.

23. (a) for the excellence of the knowledge of Christ Jesus his Lord; that he might gain Christ; (b) to know Christ and the power of His resurrection and the fellowship of His sufferings, being conformed to His death

24. (a) They saw their boldness and perceived that they were uneducated and untrained men. (b) that Peter and John had been with Jesus

25. (a) that with all boldness they might speak His word; (b) They were all filled with the Holy Spirit, and they spoke the word of God with boldness.

26. (a) to stretch out His hand to heal and to do signs and wonders through the name of Jesus; (b) Through the hands of the apostles, many signs and wonders were done among the people.

27. to preach the gospel to the poor, to heal the brokenhearted, to proclaim liberty to the captives and recovery of sight to the blind, to set at liberty those who are oppressed, and to proclaim the acceptable year of the Lord

Study 15: Earthen Vessels Chosen to Carry His Glory

Part I: The Former Glory

1. *"The glory of this latter temple shall be greater than the former."*

2. The law and the prophets

3. (a) Moses parted the Red Sea, allowing the Israelites to cross over on dry land. (b) God led the Israelites by the pillar of cloud and pillar of fire. (c) The bitter waters at Marah were made sweet.

(d) The walls of Jericho fell down, and the Israelites took the city. (e) Through the prophet Elijah, God miraculously supplied flour and oil for the widow in Zarephath. (f) Naaman was healed of leprosy. (g) A man was raised to life after touching Elisha's bones. (h) Shadrach, Meshach, and Abed-Nego's lives were preserved in the fiery furnace.

Part II: A New Dwelling Place for God's Glory

4. His glory, the glory as of the only begotten of the Father

5. "It is fitting for us to fulfill all righteousness."

6. (a)

7. "And the glory which You gave Me I have given them, that they may be one just as We are one."

8. the Day of Pentecost

Part III: The Latter Glory

9. (a) the temple of the Holy Spirit; (b) "I will dwell in them and walk among them. I will be their God, and they shall be My people."

10. a holy temple in the Lord; a dwelling place of God

11. (a) the riches of the glory; (b) in earthen vessels; (c) that the excellence of the power may be of God and not of us

12. (a) vessels of mercy; (b) glory

13. a better covenant; better promises

14. greater works than He did

Part IV: Demonstrating God's Glory on Earth

15. "Arise"

16. (a) "Awake, you who sleep, arise from the dead, and Christ will give you light." (b) "Awake"

17. (a) "shine"; (b) you shine as lights in the world

18. (a) it was the light of men; (b) rise and stand on your feet; (c) to turn them from darkness to light, and from the power of Satan to God; (d) forgiveness of sins and an inheritance among those who are sanctified by faith in Christ

19. (a) "The glory of the LORD is risen upon you." (b) the rising sun will come to us from heaven; (c) He would shine on those living in darkness and in the shadow of death. (d) The blind see, the lame walk, the lepers are cleansed, the deaf hear, the dead are raised up, and the poor have the gospel preached to them.

20. (a) His face was as the face of an angel. (b) God worked unusual miracles by Paul, including healings and the casting out of demons through handkerchiefs or aprons that had touched his body and were then brought to the sick or demon-possessed.

21. (a) Darkness will cover the earth, and deep darkness will cover the people. (b) wars and rumors of wars/nations and kingdoms fighting each other; famines; pestilences; earthquakes; tribulation; murder; hatred; offense; betrayal; false prophets bringing deception; lawlessness; the love of many grown

cold; fearful sights; great signs from heaven; (c) The gospel of the kingdom will be preached in all the world as a witness to the nations, and then the end will come. (d) to have no fellowship with them; (e) all goodness, righteousness, and truth; (f) to redeem the time, because the days are evil

22. (a) Gentiles and kings; (b) Joseph; (c) God; (d) Cornelius; (e) as a testimony to them

23. (a) Their sons shall come from afar, and their daughters shall be nursed at their side. (b) He would pour out His Spirit on their descendants and His blessings on their offspring. (c) They would all be taught by the Lord, and they would have great peace.

24. (a) the wealth of the Gentiles; (b) to ask their Egyptian neighbors for articles of silver, articles of gold, and clothing; (c) favor; what they had requested; (d) the wealth of the sinner

25. glorify the house of My glory

Study 16: Manifesting God's Glory as You Go

Part I: Called to Manifest God's Glory

1. His mighty acts and the glorious majesty of His kingdom

2. They would cast out demons, speak with new tongues, be unharmed by serpents or deadly drink, and lay hands on the sick and see them recover.

3. by His Spirit, not by might or power

Part II: A Glorious Church

4. glorious; not having spot or wrinkle or any such thing; holy and without blemish

5. (a) the glory that will be revealed in us; (b) the revealing of the sons of God

6. a far more exceeding and eternal weight of glory

7. more than conquerors

Part III: Demonstrating the Kingdom, Power, and Glory

8. (a) the kingdom, the power, and the glory; (b) "Your kingdom come. Your will be done on earth as it is in heaven."

9. doing and teaching

10. No one could do the signs that Jesus did unless God was with him.

11. forcefully

12. (a) in demonstration of the Spirit and of power; (b) with persuasive words of human wisdom; (c) so that the Corinthians' faith would not be in the wisdom of men but in the power of God

Part IV: Steps to Manifest the Glory of God Today

13. the glory of God

14. "Here am I! Send me."

15. (a) *"Go into all the world and preach the gospel to every creature."* (b) in Jerusalem, in all Judea and Samaria, and to the end of the earth

16. with great power

17. a great persecution

18. (a) He preached Christ to those in the city of Samaria. (b) He preached in all the cities until he came to Caesarea.

19. (a) Saul (Paul); (b) those in Damascus, in Jerusalem, and throughout all the region of Judea, and then the Gentiles

Part V: Demonstrate the Supernatural as You "Go"

20. heal the sick, cleanse the lepers, raise the dead, and cast out demons

21. (a) the Lord; (b) the accompanying signs

22. that the word of the Lord may run swiftly and be glorified

ABOUT THE AUTHOR

Apostle Guillermo Maldonado is a man called to bring God's supernatural power to this generation at the local and international levels. Active in ministry for over twenty years, he is the founder and pastor of Ministerio Internacional El Rey Jesús [King Jesus International Ministry]—one of the fastest-growing multicultural churches in the United States—which has been recognized for its development of kingdom leaders and for visible manifestations of God's supernatural power.

Having earned a master's degree in practical theology from Oral Roberts University and a doctorate in divinity from Vision International University, Apostle Maldonado stands firm and focused on the vision God has given him to evangelize, affirm, disciple, and send. His mission is to teach, train, equip, and send leaders and believers to bring the supernatural power of God to their communities, in order to leave a legacy of blessings for future generations. This mission is worldwide. Apostle Maldonado is a spiritual father to more than 100 pastors and apostles of local and international churches as part of a growing association, the New Wine Apostolic Network, which he founded.

He has authored many books and manuals, a number of which have been translated into several languages. His previous books with Whitaker House include *How to Walk in the Supernatural Power of God* (*Cómo Caminar en el Poder Sobrenatural de Dios*) and *The Glory of God* (*La Gloria de Dios*). In addition, he preaches the message of Jesus Christ and His redemptive power on his international television program, *Tiempo de Cambio* [*Time for Change*], which airs on several networks, thus reaching millions worldwide.

Apostle Maldonado resides in Miami, Florida, with his wife and partner in ministry, Ana, and their two sons, Bryan and Ronald.